Small Bu

INTERNET

Small Business Projects/
INTERNET

24 Projects to Revolutionize
Your Small Business

Lars D. H. Hedbor

authorHOUSE™

1663 LIBERTY DRIVE, SUITE 200
BLOOMINGTON, INDIANA 47403
(800) 839-8640
WWW.AUTHORHOUSE.COM

http://www.smallbusinessprojects.com/INTERNET/

First published by AuthorHouse 10/24/05

ISBN: 1-4208-7455-1 (e)
ISBN: 1-4208-7454-3 (sc)

Library of Congress Control Number: 2005907375

Printed in the United States of America
Bloomington, Indiana

This book is printed on acid-free paper.

for Taunya

Table of Contents

*If you've only surfed the Internet from a public library, or if you've just bought
your first PC, and are wondering what to do next, this project is a good place to
get started. It will take you through the process of signing up with a standard
dialup Internet connection. Cable modems, DSL and other options are all
explored in Project 12, later in the book.*

*Every other project in this book assumes that you have access to the Internet, so
if you don't have a connection, you should complete this project before you get
started. You could actually do some of the projects in this book without your own
computer and Internet connection, but most of them will be much harder, and
many of them will be completely impossible.*

1. Investigate the options
2. Sign up
3. Set up your email account
4. Start surfing

*Email is everywhere. Chances are you'll find an email address on nearly every
business card you see. So what happens when you add your email address to
your own cards and stationery?*

*Good email management can make your organization look more professional,
and more interested in your customer needs than many others out there. Many
businesses – small and large – fail to manage their email properly, and it costs
them their good reputation, orders, and even customers.*

*In this project, you'll lay the foundations for good practices with your customer
email for years to come. It's less about technology and more just about what is
considered to be good manners in the electronic world.*

1. A word about "spam"
2. "Netiquette"
3. Establishing an email routine
4. Acknowledge immediately, answer soon
5. Create and use templates
6. Accepting emailed orders
7. Mechanics
8. Practice, practice, practice

Table of Contents

> *It's like the old joke – "Yes, I do know everything – I just can't always remember it all." There's detailed information available online on just about any topic you can imagine, but the trick is to locate that information efficiently and quickly when you need it. This is where search engines are invaluable.*

> *It's really hard to overstate the impact that search engines can make in the way you do research. Many people who once would have turned to a bookshelf full of occasionally-used reference volumes now look first to the Internet – for nearly anything.*

1. How search engines work
2. Getting started
3. Asking the right questions
4. Sorting through the results
5. Advanced tools

> *As a small business, you are also a consumer. One of the strengths of e-commerce is its ability to efficiently serve niche markets. So, the next time you're looking for a part for your equipment, or a component for your products, or just common office supplies, try looking online.*

1. Locating suppliers
2. Online credit-card security
3. "Shipping and handling"
4. Privacy

> *When you need help with a software package, a piece of office equipment or an overdue package, you used to have only one option: hold music. And if you had a problem after business hours, you were simply out of luck. Today, however, you can turn to the Internet to increase your chances of finding the exact answer you need, and to make optimum use of your time.*

1. Check your FAQs
2. Opening the walls of their business
3. Self-service knowledge bases
4. Email for support

Every organization that participates in the marketplace leaves information about itself on the Internet. Without having to resort to one of those fraudulent "Internet SPY!!" products that spammers are so fond of hawking, you can gain critical insights into how your competition does business, what their customers think of them, and what they may be planning to do next.

One of the principles of intelligence is that you can often uncover the most closely-held secrets by simply putting together the pieces of the puzzle visible in public. Knowledge of your competitors can be gained through exercising this principle, and applying some analytical thought to the bits of information you uncover.

1. Identify your research targets
2. Study their Web site
3. Check local media
4. Check local job listings
5. Public notices
6. Newsgroup archives
7. Pulling it all together

Web-enabled e-commerce is the ultimate goal for many organizations. For a small business, getting started can be surprisingly easy. With some of the services available to online entrepreneurs, you can have a storefront up and running in no time flat.

1. Auction sites
2. Pre-built online shops
3. Shipping and handling fees
4. Taxes
5. Maintaining your reputation

One of the biggest steps you can take in opening the door to the use of the Internet in your small business is to establish your own Web site. Unfortunately, it's also where many small businesses make their biggest online mistakes. Review the Rookie Mistakes before you proceed – with any luck, you can avoid making some of these errors.

1. Register your domain name
2. Choose your content
3. Think about Web design
4. Decide who will create the site
5. Finalize design choices
6. Build the site
7. Make hosting decisions
8. Go live!
9. Mid-course adjustments
10. Change is constant

Table of Contents

"If you build it, they will come" does not necessarily apply on the Web. It's necessary to inform prospects and customers that you have a site, and to make it possible for casual browsers to find it. Fortunately, there are a lot of opportunities to promote Web sites.

Some means of driving traffic to your site are very low-cost, both in time and resources; others, if the return justifies them, can involve spending some money. This project will focus on the low-cost approaches – later projects will guide you through some of the more advanced (and spendy) ways to get the word out.

1. Get the word out
2. Understanding search engines
3. Basic searches
4. Searching by keyword
5. Pay for placement
6. Keyword Advertising
7. Links

Many small businesses use the Web to attract candidates for open positions. More job seekers than ever are turning first to the Internet to look for their next position. If they even look at traditional newspaper listings, it's just as likely to be on the newspaper's Web site. By implementing this project, you can start to attract the most qualified (and net-savvy!) candidates you've ever seen.

1. Posting on your own site
2. Using national recruiting Web sites
3. Using local online recruiting opportunities
4. Following up with candidates

One of the most interesting ways in which the Web differs from other marketing avenues is in how well you can trace your prospects' route through your content. With good traffic analysis, you can see not only which efforts are working best to drive visitors into your Web site, but you can also see how well the Web site is serving their needs.

You can also find bottlenecks that may be causing them to give up and leave. Better that you find these by looking at a few Web logs than by wondering later why your site turned out to be such a flop! By examining how your visitors navigate your site, you can help to anticipate their needs – or help them find features that they've overlooked.

1. Select and set up analysis tools
2. Understand the results
3. Act on the information

Dialup Internet access is usually sufficient for home use and is often enough when you're just getting started in business use. If you have multiple users at your place of business or if you just need to be able to use the Internet more quickly yourself, you will find yourself being tempted by the promises of greater Internet speed in various advertisements that you see.

In this project, you'll cut through the hype and decide whether a faster connection is worthwhile for your business and if so, what the benefits and drawbacks are to each of the major options available on the market today.

1. Understand the options
2. Get connected
3. Security
4. Sharing the connection
5. Employee usage
6. Internet telephony

In a business where a number of employees have their own Internet-connected computers, it makes sense to set up each of them with their own email addresses. This enables them to converse directly with customers and partners, rather than having everything go through one shared account.

When you consider that "markets are conversations," as has been observed, it makes a lot of sense to enable those conversations to take place as naturally as possible. By facilitating direct communication between your people and your customers and suppliers, you effectively extend the walls of your enterprise to encompass these people outside of your defined organization. Powerful stuff!

1. Do you need an email server?
2. Select and install email server system
3. Set up users
4. Email best practices
5. Abuse prevention

Part of the power of the Web is that it's always on – you can receive critical information from your customers even when everyone in your company is happily snoring. Setting up these important capabilities will add interactivity to your Web site, turning it into much more than just a static marketing piece.

1. Understanding Web forms
2. Building the feedback page(s)
3. Procedures for feedback
4. Extending the concept

Table of Contents

While spam is an unwelcome intruder in email inboxes everywhere, an informative, useful newsletter will nearly always get a friendly reception. Periodic newsletters also drive Web traffic and business, acting as a gentle reminder that your company stands ready to solve your customers' problems. They're also another opportunity to ask for feedback from your customers – always a good idea!

1. Getting permission
2. Creating a format
3. Generating content
4. Sending and follow-up

The "golden era" of banner advertising may be over – some contend it never arrived – but there are still opportunities to use this much-maligned advertising medium. Banner ads can be used merely to build brand awareness ("mindshare"), or to draw in very carefully targeted prospects who might not otherwise know about your company.

1. Identifying your targets
2. Common banner formats
3. Creating the banner
4. Placement
5. Follow-through and tracking

Banner ads and pay-for-placement search engine entries are not the only opportunities to get the word out on the Internet. In many cases, you can even inform potential customers about your organization's products or services by doing a public service online. As always, the trick is to not offend anyone's advertising-hostile sensibilities.

1. Third-party email newsletters
2. Email list servers
3. Search engine-related advertising

There are something in the range of 50,000 to 75,000 discussion groups active on the Internet right now. Each of these newsgroups is a vibrant community, each with its own unique quirks and rules of etiquette. One wrong word as a business can earn you an electronic black eye in these groups, but well understood and carefully used, they can be one of your most powerful means of communicating with your customers.

1. Understanding newsgroups
2. Gaining access to newsgroups
3. Finding relevant groups
4. Lurking
5. Flame wars
6. Making contributions
7. Tilt the playing field

The public newsgroups may be too raucous a place for your customers to gather and exchange information. Or, you may want to provide a private place for them to air their grievances and give input on your plans. Whatever the case may be, a customer forum can be a fascinating exercise – and one that is guaranteed to surprise you.

1. Technology and hosting options
2. Drawing an audience
3. Responding to negatives
4. Drawing on the resource

Giving your prospects the opportunity to contact you directly from your Web site can be a great use of the technology. However, it's all too easy for this to become burdensome, and an opportunity for human error to creep in. There's no need to take that risk when you can get the computer to do the dull parts of the job.

1. Building a Web form
2. Linking to the back end

Imagine being able to answer most customer questions anytime, day or night. You can make your customers and prospects happier, as well as reducing the number of late-night panicked calls you have to handle, by enabling a few simple self-help tools on your Web site.

1. Just the FAQs
2. Enabling customers to search for answers
3. Taking questions online
4. Follow-through

Table of Contents

If you have a broad inventory of products to offer, particularly if that inventory changes frequently, maintaining current and accurate information on your Web site may seem like an administrative nightmare. However, it need be no more burdensome than managing your inventory in a database.

Even better, when you can accurately communicate the state of your inventory to your customers, they will be more confident that you can fulfill their requests – or at least have a solid idea of what to expect. Setting accurate expectations is a key ingredient to great customer relationships.

1. Identifying a data source
2. Establishing a format
3. Setting expectations
4. Publishing the catalogue
5. Refreshing the catalogue

The next logical step beyond an online catalogue is to put those items on sale. There are a wide variety of approaches to this bold step into the online world. Some don't require very much risk and are not hard to implement. Others are a little harder, but offer you better control over the process.

The biggest hurdle is managing payment arrangements. This project assumes that you will want to take credit cards. If your products or services don't lend themselves to this approach, this project is worth reading anyway, since it covers some of the basics of taking customer orders on the Web, as well.

1. Accepting payment online
2. Fraud
3. Setting up a secure page
4. Security is more critical than ever
5. The shopping cart application

There are many classes of business software, such as payroll, finance, customer relationship management and so on, that have previously been available only to very large businesses, with hefty investments in infrastructure.

Many of these systems are available now to small businesses through ASPs ("application service providers"), without the need to perform complex installations, available anywhere you can get an Internet connection and for which someone else takes care of the maintenance. The availabilty of this sort of software can literally change the way you do business.

1. Understanding the technology
2. Investigate the offerings
3. Before you sign on the dotted line…

Each of these books is entertaining, insightful and will give you new ideas to extend the projects you've undertaken in this book. All of these are available from Amazon.com, BN.com and so on, and most should be available at your local bookseller.

    Search Engines
    Web Directories
    Web-Based Email
    Domain Registrars
    Site Hosting

Table of Contents

Introduction

For small businesses, the Internet has changed everything, and nothing. Opportunities far beyond a local geographical market-place are suddenly available to you; but you'll still succeed or fail on the basis of the quality of the products and services you provide to your customers. You're suddenly competing with people all over the world buzzing with ideas to "disrupt the marketplace" and "disintermediate consumers and suppliers," but a bad idea is still a bad idea, even in cyberspace.

If you've ever wondered if there's something you could be doing with the Internet but didn't know where to get started, this book is for you. Whether you're just getting started or already have an active Web site, you'll find projects in here to help your business succeed online.   It may all seem overwhelming, but it's well within your grasp. After all, if you've managed to build a success-ful business, you are certainly sharp enough to learn a few new tricks as your market evolves.

Generally speaking, each project in this book can be completed in four to eight weeks. Some are will take less time than this, and some involve long-term changes in the way you look at things. With each project, you'll see what you'll need to do before getting started, what results you might expect, how to proceed, and how to gauge your success. Some of the projects may encompass great change for your whole organization; you may be able to work on others after hours. All of them will make a difference to your business.

You don't need to read this book cover-to-cover. It's organized so that you can skip past those projects that don't apply, and get right to the ones that interest you. (You may want to review the projects you've already done, anyway, to see if they contain ideas of value to your ongoing efforts.) If you do decide to proceed from start to finish, by the time you finish with the entire book, you'll have forever changed the entire nature of your business.

I would wish you luck – but as the saying goes, "luck" is what naturally happens when opportunity meets preparedness. The opportunities abound – and this book will prepare you for them.

- Lars D. H. Hedbor

Oregon City, June 2005

Project 1:
Getting Connected for the First Time

If you've only surfed the Internet from a public library, or if you've just bought your first PC, and are wondering what to do next, this project is a good place to get started. It will take you through the process of signing up with a standard dialup Internet connection. Cable modems, DSL and other options are all explored in Project 12, later in the book.

Every other project in this book assumes that you have access to the Internet, so if you don't have a connection, you should complete this project before you get started. You could actually do some of the projects in this book without your own computer and Internet connection, but most of them will be much harder, and many of them will be completely impossible.

Prerequisites

This project requires a personal computer, modem and phone line.

Cost projections

Up to $30 per month, and 1 to 4 hours of your time.

Goals

Just getting connected to the Internet, and having an email address will probably make only a minor difference in your expenses and your revenues. You may see some intangible benefits, particularly if your customer base has been expecting you to be available online. In addition, having access to the global marketplace may enable you to find more cost-effective or convenient suppliers (see Project 4), which could help to reduce your expenses.

Procedures

1. Investigate the options

If you've just bought a PC, it's entirely possible that it came with a "free" Internet account with AOL, MSN or one of the other Internet Service Providers (ISPs). You may also have received a free CD with an offer for Internet service with a magazine in the mail or even in a box of corn flakes. (For what it's worth, spare copies of these CDs are excellent for scaring birds away from fruit trees...)

In any case, have a close look at the fine print before you sign up. Usually, the "2000 free hours" variety of offer is limited to your first month, and after that, you're paying full price. If you do the math, you'll see that it's tough to even use those 2000 "free" hours in a month's time.

At this writing, a typical unlimited-use account costs between $15 and $30 per month, with limited-use accounts from companies such NetZero available for less (some even remain free, although this is rarer than it once was). Unless you are certain that you can keep track of how long you're spending online every month, an unlimited-use account is much easier to manage.

If you don't often travel on business, you can usually save a substantial amount of money by setting up an account with a provider right in your town. On the other hand, if you're going to need a dialup connection anywhere business may take you, you should look to a national provider. Check with them to ensure that they have a local access number (also called "Point of Presence," or "POP") in each of the locations you anticipate visiting frequently. Without this, you could rack up serious long-distance charges.

It's a good idea to research ISPs on the Web – drop by your local library, go to a search site (such as Google, AltaVista, or Yahoo!), and search for "ISP." (See Project 3 for more information on using search engines.) You might even want to include your city name to narrow down the search. You'll probably find some sites that will help you to locate ISPs, as well.

If you expect to implement Project 13 and provide email addresses for your employees, you may want to look for deals that offer multiple email accounts. You should also think about the variety and volume of email you anticipate receiving, and ensure that the mailbox(es) included with your account won't limit your ability to use them for your business.

Most ISPs boast various levels of protection from "spam" - the scourge of the email inbox. Look for an offering that gives you a good level of control for dealing with spam, and doesn't just ignore the problem. See Project 2 for a more detailed look at spam, and the strategies for managing it.

Of course, there are plenty of email options available once you're online -- so don't let a poor email offering stop you from taking advantage of an otherwise attractive ISP deal.

Finally, don't worry too much about Web hosting at this stage of the game. Most hosting offered as part of a basic dial-up package is geared toward personal sites, rather than business usage. Review Project 8 to get a better idea of what you'll be looking for once you're ready to build your own Web site, especially if the plan you're considering claims to include business-quality hosting.

Other features to look for include newsgroup access (see Project 18 for a description of newsgroups), as well as future availability of a faster broadband connection (see Project 12); if you can simply switch on higher speed without having to change providers, the transition will be much less painful. (You may want to consider just leaping right in and starting with a broadband connection. Let your cash flow and anticipation of implementing some of the advanced projects in this book guide your decision.)

You may also want to check with your local business development organizations to see what information they may have available on

ISPs in your area.

2. Sign up

Once you've decided on an ISP, it's time to go ahead and sign up. You will probably have a CD-ROM with their software on it. There may also be a temporary account name and password on the materials you have. Ensure that the modem is plugged into a phone line, and then start the software installation, following the directions with the package.

Nearly all ISPs will either require prepayment or a credit card, which they'll automatically bill on a monthly basis. If you're entering your credit card on a Web page, be sure that it's on a secure site – look for the lock or key icon in the bottom of the window displayed by your Web browser (the software that you use to access the Web, such as Microsoft Internet Explorer, Mozilla Firefox, Opera or Netscape Navigator). See Project 4 for more information about using your credit card on the Web.

Some ISPs will allow you to sign up over the phone, and they'll then send you any software and access information you'll need via the mail. If you're more comfortable with this, by all means take advantage of it. However, if you're motivated by instant gratification, you may find it very difficult to wait for the postman!

3. Set up your email account

During the signup, you'll probably have the opportunity to set up your email account. Typically, you'll have the chance to choose the first part of your address – the "yourname" part of "yourname@someisp.com." You can use letters and numbers, but no spaces or punctuation. Do try to choose something that you can share easily, such as over the phone, and that your business associates can remember. Most people use their business name or something based on their own name.

You may not be able to get your first choice, particularly if it's based on a common name such as John Smith, or Acme Services. You may have to try multiple account names, particularly with national ISPs. Keep in mind that you'll be using this address for your business – "pinkiebear@someisp.com" may not be appropriate for a sporting-goods shop, even though it may very well be available.

Many ISPs offer the option of multiple email addresses on a single account. This gives you more flexibility, and so it may be worth looking for, if you think you may need addresses for other than just business use. (You will not usually need to set the other addresses up right away, so don't worry too much about this capability if it is part of the offer you select.)

4. Start surfing

If you haven't spent much time on the Web yet, it's a good idea for you to do so now. The more experience you have in browsing the Internet, the more ideas you'll get about using it. Look around for things that might be of interest – sites that cater to your hobbies, for example, or suppliers with whom you already do business.

Explore the capabilities of your Web browser. Most browsers offer the ability to keep track of sites that you'd like to visit again, by use of "bookmarks" or "favorites." Some permit you to view your history, so that you can have another look at that fascinating page you saw last Tuesday. Read the documentation and learn what the browser can enable you to do.

Learn to use search engines; Project 3 will guide you through this illuminating experience.

Assessing Results

How many times in a week do you give out your email address now? How much email do you send and receive for your business? How many hours do you save by searching for a part with a simple online query instead of flipping through a catalogue? The answers to these questions will help you to gauge how much of an impact this project has had on your business.

What's Next?

Now that you have an email account, you'll have the opportunity to have your customers communicate with you via email. It's critical that you understand the protocols and expectations that are associated with the use of email in business dealings. Project 2 will serve as an introduction to customer email management.

If you've not yet had the pleasure of learning how to find what you're seeking by the use of search engines, then Project 3 is a must – it will help you find resources you only dreamed could be available before now.

The Internet is ideal for checking up on your competition. There's a wealth of information to be gleaned from the presence of any organization on the Web, and it's always a good idea to know what the other guy's up to. Project 6 gives you some guidelines and ideas to use in competitive research on the Internet.

Continue to familiarize yourself with the resources available to you on the Web. You'll probably get a lot of ideas for ways to use the Internet yourself – keep a notebook, or bookmark your favorites for later reference. Bear in mind that the Internet changes constantly – so a page you bookmark today may be gone the next time you try to look at it.

Congratulations on joining the Internet revolution – you've just taken a first step that will likely change your entire way of doing business!

Project 2:
Managing Customer Email

Email is everywhere. Chances are you'll find an email address on nearly every business card you see. So what happens when you add your email address to your own cards and stationery?

Good email management can make your organization look more professional, and more interested in your customer needs than many others out there. Many businesses – small and large – fail to manage their email properly, and it costs them their good reputation, orders and even customers.

In this project, you'll lay the foundations for good practices with your customer email for years to come. It's less about technology and more just about what is considered to be good manners in the electronic world.

Prerequisites

You will need an email account, preferably on your own Internet-connected computer. You will also need to know how to use your email software. Consult the manuals or on-line help if you need to learn about the software. You could start this project with just a Web-based email account on a site such as www.gmail.com, www.hotmail.com or www.yahoo.com, but you will be much more able to manage your email with specialized software on your own computer.

Cost projections

1 to 5 hours per week of your time, depending upon the volume of email you send and receive.

There are no additional financial costs for this project, once you have some sort of email account, and (optionally) email software on your computer.

Goals

Because email tends to accelerate communications, you may see a reduction in the length of your sales cycle, as well as a potential decrease in the age of your receivables. You may also want to watch your average order size and repeat business numbers, as well. Good email practices tend to promote customer loyalty.

If you keep track of your customers' geographic data, this is another measurement that will likely change as you start using email. If you ship mail-ordered goods, you may see some boosts to this side of your business, though there are some special considerations that we'll discuss below.

Procedures

1. A word about "spam"

You've probably seen the emails offering to send your message to millions of potential customers. Don't fall for this, for the love of your reputation. You've probably also gotten some emails offering you certain less tasteful services – which did not interest you at all. These are known as "spam" (a name derived from a well-known Monty Python sketch), and are the bane of email inboxes everywhere.

If you employ the method of sending unsolicited email, not only are you blasting your message out just as indiscriminately as the pornographers and scammers, but you're also putting yourself in their company. In addition, there can be other, more serious consequences – such as fines in some jurisdictions, the potential for Federal criminal penalties and, frequently, the loss of your Internet service. There's no excuse for spam – don't become part of the problem.

After you've had an email address for a while, the spammers are likely to discover it and start sending to it. If you find yourself being inundated in spam, there are only a few substantive things that you can do. First of all, you need to be able to recognize what is and is not spam. Spam is sometimes referred to as "UCE" ("unsolicited commercial email"). It's typically sent via automated systems that spew out thousands or even millions of messages per day.

Since email costs nothing to send (beyond a connection to the Internet), there's no particular incentive for spammers to bother filtering for their target market. They don't care which addresses might have a potential customer for pornography, illegitimate college "degrees" or Viagra, and which ones belong to 9-year-old children whose parents will suddenly have to explain some difficult topics.

Emails from a company to which you've voluntarily given your email address are not usually considered spam. Some of the hallmarks of spam are nonsense "from" addresses, "to" addresses other than your email address, tracking identification numbers or codes in the subject or body and URLs made up of numbers or other apparent gobbledegook to "protect" their location.

Both spam and legitimate messages may well bear notices that you were subscribed by your own action and links to email addresses or Web sites where you can be removed from their list. You should *never* reply to spam. If you don't recall subscribing to an email newsletter, don't unsubscribe – just toss it. Replying in any way to spam just verifies that someone's using the email address, which will land you on a hot list for more spam.

Of course, it goes without saying that you should *never*, but *never* purchase something from a spammer. Rewarding their knavery will only encourage them, and any legitimate product you want can be bought from a more respectful – and respectable – merchant.

There is an emerging class of technologies designed to combat spam, both keeping it out of your specific mailbox, and taking steps to actually impose some form of cost on the act of sending large numbers of messages.

Spam blocking software typically looks for messages which "look like" spam. With varying degrees of accuracy, it usually attempts to selectively mark those messages for later disposal. The risk here, of course, is that the software simply does not possess human understanding of the content or context of messages.

As a result, it may cast too wide a net – and wind up snaring legitimate messages along with the garbage. Be sure to periodically look over the messages labeled as "spam" to ensure that you're not throwing out the baby with the bath water.

The software improves constantly, but so, of course, do the spammers, learning how to trick the systems into thinking that their messages should be delivered. Many systems can be configured as well – it's worth reading up a bit on yours to make it work as well as possible.

There are many sites on the Web that cover the ever-changing methods that spammers use, and explain how to counter them. Some of the best sites are www.cauce.org, www.spamcop.net and www.samspade.org. Considering that you've spent your company dollars on Internet connectivity, you may find it worth a little bit of time to learn how to prevent others from hijacking your email inbox.

2. "Netiquette"

As in other areas of human interaction, there is a definite etiquette that's been established for email. Most are a simple extension of good manners in normal human interaction – don't "shout" (i.e., type in ALL CAPITAL LETTERS), do take the time to calm down before firing off an angry message, and always keep in mind that your words can come back to haunt you. These practices and others are sometimes known as "netiquette" (net etiquette).

There can and have been entire books written about netiquette – if you'd like to learn more about it, do a quick lookup on your favorite search engine or browse through your local bookstore. This would be a good opportunity for you to try online commerce, too – some of the best bookstores in the world are now online – www.amazon.com, www.bn.com, and others all have listings for books on netiquette. (See Project 4 for more information about shopping online.)

3. Establishing an email routine

Research has shown that a shockingly large number of organizations *never* reply to email inquiries – and even more reply only after an unreasonable delay. Fortunately, it's very easy to establish good email habits, which may well set you apart from your competitors.

At a bare minimum, check your email daily. It's commonly expected that a business will reply to an email inquiry within one working day – if you can reply more quickly than that, you'll look all the more on top of things. Budget some time – put it on your schedule if you have trouble remembering to do it – to respond to email every business day.

4. Acknowledge immediately, answer soon

If someone sends a complex question – one that's going to take some research – acknowledge their email with a quick message, ideally giving them an idea of when they can expect a full answer from you. Whenever possible, make answering those questions a priority – as you already know, someone who's asking tough questions is usually satisfying their last doubts just prior to placing an order.

5. Create and use templates

Many of the email inquiries you receive will have common themes. You can create templated answers, and then use those templates to quickly answer many of your emails. This will not only save you time but will also ensure consistency. It can also be a terrific approach if you have several people sharing the responsibility for answering email.

If you do use this method, be sure to always personalize your answer in some way – it will let your correspondents know that a person, rather than a machine, handled their question. It's interesting to note that even some Fortune 100 companies use this method, and in some of these cases, one person is able to answer the bulk of the massive volumes of email they receive with a personal - but "canned" - reply.

Other large companies use software systems to attempt to manage their email. You can usually tell the difference – and you're sure to get a sense of which companies value their customers more.

6. Accepting emailed orders

You can certainly accept orders via email. However, be wary of asking your customers to send you credit-card numbers in email. The nature of most email transmissions leaves open the potential for people to read them as they're routed from the sender's machine to yours. The analogy that's been made most often is that normal email is like a postcard – any interested party along the way can read anything in them.

While it is possible to secure email so that it is very difficult for a third party to snoop into it, the means to do so are not yet widely deployed. Unless you're serving a very savvy audience, they're not likely to be willing or able to set up their email to be secure enough that you should accept their credit-card information by that medium.

Some businesses get around this problem by simply accepting the order online, and then arranging payment via a follow-up phone call. Alternatively, if the nature of your business is such that you'd ordinarily bill on net 30 days, you can extend that practice to emailed orders without disruption. This will be especially true when you're dealing with existing customers.

Make sure that any customers who will be placing orders via email know what information you'll need in order to fulfill their requests. You may even want to put together an email template that you can send to new customers that they can fill out and return to you, secure in the knowledge that their order will be placed without delay.

7. Mechanics

Your email software may include the ability to append a "sig" (signature block) to the end of your messages. Even if you don't use this capability, it's almost always a good idea to end each message with your name, email address, and even your telephone number. (Once you have a Web site, you'll want to include its address, as well.)

Work to use a conversational, but not necessarily chummy, tone of voice in your email. Since some of your customers and prospects may only know you through your on-line interactions, it's important that you put your best foot forward.

If you know that you have weaknesses in your spelling or grammar, make sure that you take advantage of the spell-check and grammar review tools in many modern email packages. Bear in mind that these tools are far from perfect, though. Particularly as you develop your email templates, you may want to have someone with great grammar and spelling skills review them.

A word of caution is justified here – it's very easy to send an email that is misinterpreted, leading to anger on all sides. Always re-read your messages before you send them, looking for both grammar and spelling errors and for the larger mistakes that are all too common in electronic communications.

Remember, if you're feeling angry as you write, set it aside until you calm down – or refrain from ever sending it. If there's a personal attack, eliminate it. If the tone is confrontational or defensive, re-write it. Remember that with email, your words can and will come back to haunt you with remarkable ease and longevity.

8. Practice, practice, practice

Establish email conversations with your family and friends – you'll learn more by actually using email than you ever could by reading about it. You'll gain a first-hand appreciation of the usefulness of this new medium and a deeper understanding of how it differs – or is similar – to the ways you've communicated in the past.

Assessing Results

After a month or two, you may begin to see some of the business metrics you've chosen start to move in the direction you desired. Sales cycle length will impact your cost of sales (less of your time invested in a given sale reduces your expense). Increased customer loyalty will likely result in improved top-line revenues.

You may also find that you're gaining new insights by being able to review your archived messages from your customers. Having your conversations recorded in one place, where there's less opportunity for confusion, and with the ability to search and sort them, will be a resource for any dispute resolution that becomes necessary over time, too.

What's Next?

Continue to foster good relations with your customers via this communications medium – your efforts now will yield dividends that will surprise you over the long run. As you gain a reputation for being responsive, polite and professional in your electronic communications, your business will benefit from the word-of-mouth (or should that be word-of-keyboard?) referrals that will result.

Now that you've established some basic email habits, you can start to consider how to use email in other ways. You will establish Internet email accounts for all of your employees in Project 13 – make sure that they all apply the lessons of this project when you do. Project 15 will guide you through establishing an email newsletter. In Project 18, which discusses newsgroups, you'll use many of these same skills to communicate with people in these forums.

Project 3:
Learning to Use Search Engines

It's like the old joke – "Yes, I *do* know everything – I just can't always remember it all." There's detailed information available online on just about any topic you can imagine, but the trick is to locate that information efficiently and quickly when you need it. This is where search engines are invaluable.

It's really hard to overstate the impact that search engines can make in the way you do research. Many people who once would have turned to a bookshelf full of occasionally-used reference volumes now look first to the Internet – for nearly anything.

Prerequisites

This project requires that you have access to the Internet; of course, if it's via your own computer, with your own connection, you may be more comfortable.

Cost projections

Expect to spend a few hours of your time learning the quirks and tricks of using search engines in general. After that, the amount of time you'll spend is limited only by your research needs – and your curiosity.

There are no additional financial costs involved in using search engines.

Goals

Upon completing this project, you should be able to find resources to help you answer nearly any question you can contemplate.

1. How search engines work

Search engines largely solve what the respected science fiction
author Robert Heinlein expected to be the greatest crisis of the
information age – the difficulty of cataloging and synthesizing
the knowledge we're generating at rates approaching exponential
growth. Consider the magnitude of the feat: tracing billions
of pages of content connected by a tenuous and ever-changing
network of linkages, extracting the essential nature of each of
those pages, and then responding to searches with material that's
even vaguely related to your request. Search engines are some
incredible technology!

However, these feats pretty much break down into simple individual tasks, each performed many, many times, very quickly.
That's the sort of problem that computers are designed to address,
and search engines just make those solutions available to us all.

First, most search engines start with a piece of software that
"crawls" the Web, following the links found on one page to the
next page, then following the links on that page, and so on. Along
the way, this software generally captures a snapshot of the content
on each page (methods and quantities of content captured vary) to
search against.

This content is very efficiently indexed, again using a variety of
methods. When you send in a search request, the search engines
select a set of responses that match your search in one way or
another (once again, methods vary). Finally, the search engines
rank the results they're presenting according to their relevance to
your request. (This last step is where the really advanced work is
done, ensuring that you can quickly get to the answer you were
looking for.)

2. Getting started

There are a number of very good search engines available on the
Internet, at no charge to you. Most are supported in some way or
another by advertising, which means that the competition is keen

to provide the best possible search results, so that users will come back again and again.

As of this writing, the undisputed champion in the search engine market is www.google.com, although www.altavista.com and www.hotbot.com were each pioneers at earlier stages of the technology's development. Other entrants to keep an eye on as the market matures include search.yahoo.com and www.msn. com, as well as Amazon's www.a9.com (which is currently in part based on Google's technology).

Of course, these are just a few of the dozens of search engines vying for your usage. If you prefer to see results from a number of search engines presented all together, you can try www.mamma. com. If you like to ask questions in full English sentences, you can do so at www.ask.com. It's largely a matter of personal preference.

In any event, start by launching your browser and surfing to the home page of the search engine you want to try. Start by entering your own name, and submit the search. If you have a common name, you may get hundreds or thousands of matches, none of which have anything to do with you.

You may also find references to yourself, perhaps from news accounts, or from online communities you've participated in at one time or another. This can be a very interesting exercise, and it may give you some insight into what you may expect to find when you start researching your competitors (see Project 6 for more information).

3. Asking the right questions

As you may have seen in this first search, entering common terms can give you an unwieldy number of results to sift through. On the other hand, entering very unusual terms may give you no results at all – which is potentially even more useless.

There are a couple of general guidelines to bear in mind, though each search engine will have a link somewhere on the page to helpful hints on how to get the most out of that particular engine.

Unless you're using a plain-English search engine, (also known as a "natural language" search), you will want to leave out common words: "the," "and," "of" and so forth. Most search engines will throw these words out automatically, since nearly any page written in English would show up in your search results otherwise. If there's no need to type them, drop them.

If you're searching on a multi-word term, enclose it in quotes. This way, if you're looking for pages regarding "Bob Smith Plumbing," you won't get pages where those three words show up just anywhere – Bob Davis commenting on a clog in the Smith's sink, for example.

As mentioned in Project 4, if you're looking for a very specific part, search engines can be brilliant at finding references to items by part number. Since these tend to be seen as "words" when the search engines scan online catalogues or similar content, they often make for very good search terms.

4. Sorting through the results

So you enter your question, and the Web page comes back showing the first 20 possible matches… of 1,893. Don't despair; these matches are typically sorted so that the pages most likely to be relevant to your question appear at the top of the list.

There's usually some form of abstract or extract from the page, often showing you exactly what terms were found on it, so that you can gauge its usefulness in answering your question. However, there's often nothing to do but to click over to the page and look at it for yourself.

If the search engine doesn't do it for you automatically, open the link in a new window, so that you don't lose your results page. (Typically, this is done by clicking the alternate button on your mouse, or by some other keyboard/mouse combination; see your browser's help file for details.) Otherwise, you may catch yourself closing the browser window, and losing the ability to use the back button to return to your search results.

Many times, your results set may come back in a multitude of languages. Don't discount these entirely, even if you don't speak the languages. Many times, sites will have prominent links to equivalent content in English, or you may be able to puzzle out what the page means by cognates.

Too, some search engines can make a try at machine translation for you. These translations probably wouldn't get you a passing grade in your high school Spanish class, but they are usually adequate to get the gist of the page's content.

5. Advanced tools

In addition to searching content on Web pages, many search engines offer other useful abilities. Some can search for images (typically matching on text around them and the images' file names), others search newsgroup archives (which will be very useful to you in Project 18), and some search through online catalogues. Explore these capabilities in each of the major search engine offerings as you familiarize yourself with their capabilities.

One of the more innovative applications of searching technologies is presented by Google at news.google.com. Here, you can get an automatically-generated rundown of the day's news, or you can search for specific terms in the news.

Even more useful, you can have the system watch the news articles as it gathers them and email you an alert whenever a new story appears containing your chosen terms. This has the powerful effect of serving as a global news clipping service, which can give you immediate notice of developments of importance to you. This truly is a wonderful age!

New technologies are always appearing as the "arms race" between the search providers escalates. As consumers of information, we all benefit from this robust competition, and from the support of the advertisers for these tools.

Assessing Results

You should notice that you're spending less time doing research in paper books and magazines, and not needing to go to your library as often to answer questions in both your business and in your personal life.

Your increased efficiency may be partially offset by an increasing urge to satisfy your curiosity about a wide array of topics; you will need to find your own balance on this score!

What's Next?

Now that you've gained an understanding of one of the primary means of navigating the Internet, you're ready to take on a range of tasks. You can start by trying out some e-commerce, in Project 4, and you now have most of the tools to start doing in-depth competitive research, in Project 6.

Project 4:
Shopping Online

As a small business, you are also a consumer. One of the strengths of e-commerce is its ability to efficiently serve niche markets. So, the next time you're looking for a part for your equipment, or a component for your products, or just common office supplies, try looking online.

Prerequisites

You must have Internet access in order to shop online. For most sites, you will also need to have a credit card and a valid shipping address. (For example, many e-commerce sites ship only via UPS or FedEx, neither of which delivers to post office boxes.)

Cost projections

The idea of this project is not to go shop online just for its own sake, but to use it as an opportunity to save money for your business. In addition to cash savings, the efficiency of shopping right from your desk, rather than having to travel to and then hunt through a physical store should result in a net savings of time.

Goals

During the course of this project, the entire focus will be on reducing your overhead. Every time you have to go on a shopping trip, page through a paper catalogue, or – worst of all – go without a crucial item, it has an impact on your bottom line.

Procedures

1. Locating suppliers

The Internet offers a new opportunity to decrease your costs. In some cases, you will simply be able to locate an unusual component more quickly. In other cases, the Web will permit you to place a routine order with an existing supplier more efficiently. You may also find far more competitive suppliers for certain items than you have available in your local market.

Of course, most small business proprietors have a vested interest in doing business within their communities. By no means should the Internet override the reasons for this conscious choice. Severing long-standing business relationships for a matter of a few dollars is usually a bad overall business decision.

On the other hand, you may be eager to find alternatives to some of the merchants and suppliers with whom you deal. The Internet shatters many effective monopolies, leveling the playing field for small businesses in ways that nobody had foreseen.

You probably have office equipment that takes specific supplies and maintenance parts. You may have had to sit on the phone with the manufacturer's hold music, waiting to talk to a salesperson who then tried to push an expensive add-on or talk you into replacing the entire unit.

Now, you can simply note the part number, and go to your favorite search engine. Enter the part number and perhaps the name of the manufacturer (including the word "sale" may also be a good idea), and you'll probably get a whole list of Web sites, each of which is vying for your business.

Google has launched a search engine specifically geared to search online catalogs, which is available at www.froogle.com. This resource may be worth examining, as it allows you to filter and sort by price, as well as by supplier. Other sites that provide similar services include www.mysimon.com, www.epinions.com, and, specializing in technology items, www.pricewatch.com.

Of course, the manufacturer can still serve as a resource – look up its Web site, and there may well be a list of authorized online retailers, with links you can use to jump right to these suppliers. Or, if the manufacturer is the only supplier of a given part, it may be set up to allow you to purchase right online – no more hold music or pushy salespeople.

If you're looking for a broader class of items, you can enter related "keywords" – a word or two that comprises a general description of the item – and have a list of online vendors to choose from.

Like any other mail-order business, online retailing (also known as "e-commerce") can usually achieve savings by eliminating the need for sales personnel highly trained to separate you from your money, as well as the polished physical facilities designed to impress and assist visitors.

Some markets that have been notably well served by the growth of e-commerce include travel, books, music, computers and their supplies, general office supplies and highly specialized items. In particular, those items where there may be only one or two suppliers anywhere are now more readily and inexpensively available than ever before. If you're nursing along an older piece of equipment, this applies very much to its needs for parts and supplies.

2. Online credit-card security

Many users of e-commerce sites suffer a twinge of uncertainty as they see a blank where they're expected to enter their credit card number and then send it hurtling into cyberspace. In most cases, this anxiety is misplaced, but there are a few common-sense guidelines to follow.

Most important is that the pages accepting any sort of critically private information – personal medical history, financial, many password-access pages – are transmitted with the assurance of encryption. Your Web browser will usually have some sort of visual indicator – Netscape Navigator displays a key icon (small picture), Internet Explorer uses a lock, and other browsers will have their own standards. (Check your Web browser's help file, looking for the term "SSL" or "security" for more information.)

Once the vendor has your credit card, it is responsible for safe-guarding the information. There have been unfortunate cases of hackers gaining access to sensitive data on the poorly secured systems of irresponsible vendors, but in most cases, the damage has been minimal.

As always, examine your credit card statement closely, and imme-diately report any charges you don't recognize. Most credit card issuers will only hold you liable for the first $50 or so of fraudu-lent charges, and some have reduced your liability in the case of online fraud to zero. In most cases, you must report fraudulent activity promptly, or you may wind up being held responsible for the charges anyway. Check with your issuer for details.

3. "Shipping and handling"

Many mail-order businesses offer what appear to be great prices, until you reach the end of the process and realize that they're making up the difference in inflated shipping charges and "handling" fees that you would think should just be part of their overhead.

Sadly, this practice is rampant online, as well. Shop carefully, and if you find that a site is clearly charging in excess of actual ship-ping costs, take your business elsewhere. If you are so moved, you can send them an email informing them of your decision, and explaining that they may be able to earn your business once they stop looking at their shipping department as a profit center.

Most leading e-commerce sites give you the shipping and han-dling charges early in the ordering process, although some don't tell you what the total will be until after you've supplied most of your personal information. The best e-commerce sites let you see your shipping and handling charges right up front, even before you supply anything more detailed than your ZIP or postal code.

Many sites will quote "free shipping," particularly with a mini-mum order size - but be sure that you're getting the best overall price for your items. Remember, "there ain't no such thing as a free lunch." Someone's always paying the price, somehow.

4. Privacy

Once you share your personal information with any merchant - online or not - that information can be used to improve their marketing efforts. Most online merchants have a privacy statement that details how and when your personal information may be used — and how to tell them that you don't want it used.

Look out for the sneaky practice of subscribing your email address to their marketing communications by default. Worse, some sites even presume that you're happy to have your email address shared with their "marketing partners." (This is usually a phrase that means "anyone willing to pay for a list of email addresses.") A checkbox that's already checked off should be a red flag — read what you're agreeing to by leaving it checked!

If you find that this has happened to you, try to determine which merchant has done this to you, and call them on it! There's a chance that they will respond to enough customer pressure, and change their practices. And, of course, let them know that they won't get any more business from you. If you're certain about a merchant's unacceptable practices, and they refuse to change, you may even want to warn others, leveraging your influence throughout your circle of associates.

Assessing Results

This will be easy. Consider the difference in the costs, both financial and in terms of time saved by shopping online, as compared to the old way. The difference should be a reduction in your business expenses - and you can carry that straight to the bottom line.

What's Next?

If you'd like to see what the market has to say about a particular merchant, or share your experiences, Internet newsgroups may be an invaluable resource for you. Project 18 will show you how to get started with these communities.

After a while, you may start wondering whether you could do a better job of selling on the Internet. Project 7 will get you started, and Projects 21 and 22 will move you further along the path to serving your own customers – wherever they may be.

Project 5:
Getting Support Via the Internet

When you need help with a software package, a piece of office equipment or an overdue package, you used to have only one option: hold music. And if you had a problem after business hours, you were simply out of luck. Today, however, you can turn to the Internet to increase your chances of finding the exact answer you need, and to make optimum use of your time.

Prerequisites

You must have Internet access in order to work on this project. While you could work through it with a hypothetical problem, you'll learn a lot more with a real issue to solve.

Cost projections

It may take you as long as an hour or so to research and solve your first problem using the resources described in this project. After that, you'll be more comfortable using the Internet to research support questions, so you'll have a greater net savings of time.

Goals

You will see increased efficiency, reduced frustration and a lower incidence of hold music-induced earaches. You'll also have a greater sense of independence from the knowledge that you can usually find the answers to your support questions on your own.

As you use the resources that different companies put on the Internet to enable self-support, watch for things that work particularly well. In Project 21, you'll have an opportunity to use the best examples of self-support you've encountered as inspiration as you build online self-support tools for your customers.

Procedures

1. Check your FAQs

FAQs ("frequently asked questions"; the acronym is variously pronounced either "fak" or spelled out: "F-A-Q") usually consist of a question-and-answer formatted document that organizations put on their Web sites to resolve the most common queries they receive from their customers. They're usually prominently posted on a company's Web site, sometimes under the "support" section, but sometimes right on the home page.

If you don't see an obvious link directing you to the FAQ listing, try using any site map or index that's provided. Or, if there's a search capability on the site, enter the search term "FAQ" there.

Failing that, depart the company Web site for the moment and go to your favorite search engine. Enter the product name or company name (if the company has only a few products) and the search term "FAQ" and see what may be available on the entire Web.

If you do come up with an FAQ listing, scan through the questions to see whether one of them appears to pertain to your issue. If so, try the remedy suggested. If this solves your problem, you've just saved yourself a frustrating exercise in old-style customer support.

It's reasonably likely that the FAQ will answer your question. But if there's no listing available, or if your issue doesn't appear to be covered, we can move right along to the next level of sophistication in online self-support.

2. Opening the walls of their business

Many organizations make a wide variety of information about your dealings with them available to you over the Internet. One simple example is package tracking. All of the major shipping companies offer online tools to find out where your item is, and when you can expect to receive it. When you placed an order in Project 4, you may have received a tracking number, or even a direct link to the tracking site.

Other examples of this capability include ordering history at e-commerce sites, account balances, issue tracking (see Step 4, below) and much more. This can sometimes include very detailed information about your relationship with the organization. Typically, this information is well-protected and requires you to log in.

You may have to request an online account by telephone or by mail, particularly with systems that give you access to very sensitive information, such as online banking and other financial sites. Other sites may permit you to establish an account right online, by providing information from a bill or other authenticating data.

3. Self-service knowledge bases

Within many support organizations, there is a set of answers to the problems that the support analysts see over and over again. These answers may take the form of a binder with flow-charted solution trees, or they may be in an electronic knowledge base of some sort.

A lot of companies have realized that their customers can search a knowledge base almost as quickly as a support analyst can, so they've put the knowledge bases on the Internet, freeing up the analysts to tackle the tougher questions.

Everybody wins in this scenario. Customers are better served, since they can solve the easy questions at their own convenience, while the hard questions get faster attention from a skilled analyst. The company wins, since it achieves a higher level of customer satisfaction and reduces the high staff turnover rates associated with repetitive, uninspiring support call center positions.

If the company from which you need help enlightened in this manner, you can try out its online knowledge base. Typically, these operate as a miniature search engines, whose results are drawn from the text and concepts of just the set of issues and answers the company has published (as opposed to the entire Web examined by a full-blown search engine).

Look within the company's support section on its Web site. You can also try the site map or index, just as you did when you were looking for the FAQ document. Alternatively, many companies give the address to their knowledge base Web page within the hold music when you call for support.

Once you've located the knowledge base search page, you can enter keywords regarding the problem you're having. The system will return a list of potential answers, often with some form of relevance score associated with each answer. If you've done a search with very specific terms (a part number or an error message), this relevance information can be a good guide to the likelihood of the answer actually answering your question. For broader searches, the usefulness of the score can be pretty low.

As before, when you find an answer that appears to pertain to your problem, follow the suggested steps to resolve it. If the problem persists, it's time for "Plan B."

4. Email for support

Emailing a support analyst is likely to still be a better use of your time than picking up the phone. All of the advantages of email that you learned about in Project 2 pertain. In particular, clarity and scheduling convenience make support email a good choice – again, both for you and for the firm involved.

When you send an email to a support organization, remember to clearly state your issue. List any steps that you've already taken to resolve it. If you can, give them information that will help them to reproduce the problem.

If you're upset about the issue, strive to keep your irritation out of the message – remember that the recipient is on your side, and typically has incentives to resolve your question as quickly as possible.

In many cases, you'll find an online form to send in your question. It's a good idea to take advantage of these, because they often ensure that you supply all of the information that the support staff will need, and may also interface with support automation tools within the organization, which increases the efficiency of managing your question.

You may get an immediate acknowledgment, often with some sort of a reference number for you to use if you need to add to your original request, or follow up on it in some other way. In most cases, this acknowledgment will also give you some idea of what to expect in terms of a response time.

Sometimes, you may even get a list of possible solutions returned to you immediately, by systems that are close kin to the knowledge base search tools you tried earlier. Do have a look at any suggestions you receive through this avenue – the greater detail in your emailed description of the issue, or a difference in the systems used to search for an answer may yield the correct answer through this mechanism.

Once you've received an answer that resolves the problem, be sure to let the support staff know that they can close your record. Some support organizations have policies that require positive verification that a problem's been resolved, and the analyst's time is better spent researching the next issue than in repeatedly trying to contact you to close the problem.

Assessing Results

You should see reduced downtime, resultant improvements in morale and greater efficiency. These benefits will accrue wherever you can solve simple problems in the everyday course of running your business.

What's Next?

You've probably noted some ideas of things to do on your own Web site, when the time comes. While most customer self-support systems are more complex than you probably want to tackle in your first Web site effort, you might still take a peek at Project 21, which discusses enabling customer self-support on your Web site.

If you don't have a Web site yet, between this project, Project 4's online shopping, and the competitive research of Project 6, you may be developing some really good ideas about what you'd like to do on your site. Proceed to Project 8 to start on that exciting effort.

Project 6:
Studying the Competition

Every organization that participates in the marketplace leaves information about itself on the Internet. Without having to resort to one of those fraudulent "Internet SPY!!" products that spammers are so fond of hawking, you can gain critical insights into how your competition does business, what their customers think of them, and what they may be planning to do next.

One of the principles of intelligence is that you can often uncover the most closely-held secrets by simply putting together the pieces of the puzzle visible in public. Knowledge of your competitors can be gained through exercising this principle, and applying some analytical thought to the bits of information you uncover.

Competitive intelligence is an entire discipline, with skilled practitioners and detailed codes of conduct. If this is an activity that you find will make a large difference in your business results, you might do well to consult some of the literature around this field. Again, a visit to your local bookstore or to one of the fine Web sites selling books will help you tap into the wealth of information on this topic.

Prerequisites

You'll need a personal computer with an Internet connection and a good understanding of the use of search engines (see Project 3). Some knowledge of how to read financial statements may be helpful, as well.

Cost projections

You will spend around 5 to 10 hours per competitor, although you may decide to spend more time on key business rivals. Maintaining this valuable repository of knowledge will probably take you an hour or so per month for each competitor.

Goals

This project's results may be somewhat difficult to quantify, but some of the metrics to watch may include competitive loss numbers, with particular attention to trends in the losses to those competitors whom you've been studying. As a result of decreasing competitive losses, you may see changes in your gross sales numbers. This measure may also be affected by your ability to react quickly to your competitors' initiatives.

You will be able to train new sales staff more quickly, as well as being able to refresh your own memory, with a dossier for each of your major competitors in hand. This will also have an impact on your sales effectiveness, particularly if you have a high turnover rate among your sales personnel.

Procedures

1. Identify your research targets

If you've been formally tracking sales opportunity losses to your competitors, selecting targets for research is as simple as figuring out who's been the most effective against you in head-to-head competition. Otherwise, you might try asking a few trusted customers where else they might shop for the goods and services you provide.

You might also try doing an Internet search as if you were in the market for your own goods or services. If your company provides something that can be easily shipped, this will probably be very easy. If it's something that has to be provided in person, you may still find that there's someone in your market who's been using the Internet to solicit business effectively — from your customers!

To start, pick just three to five of your top competitors to study intensively. Each of these will consume at least several hours of your time, so choose carefully.

2. Study their Web site

If your chosen competitor has a Web site, that's a great place to start. This is where they'll present themselves as they want their customers to see them. The most interesting and useful information you may find on a competitor's Web site will be price lists and product data sheets. If they have enabled online shopping, you should be able to verify current prices there. Indeed, if your budget extends far enough, you might even consider buying the competitor's products online. (Ship them to your home address.)

Note their shipping policies, and if you do make a purchase from them, check to see whether their promised performance is met. Since shipping is one of the major differences between purchasing most products online versus buying them in a physical store, many customers are particularly sensitive to unreasonable expenses or delays.

If they've posted press releases, you can start to assemble an organization chart, as nearly every press release includes quotes from high-ranking company officials. Press releases will also help you to understand very well how the company wants to be seen by the media and by its customers. The company will usually include some form of their basic mission statement, as well as an idea of why they feel they're different from (and better than) their competition — namely, you.

If they have job postings listed, these can give you a detailed view of what holes they have in their organization at the moment. In addition, the skills required can give you great insight into what their future plans might be.

For instance, a retail shop advertising for full-time equipment service positions may be planning an expansion into that market. Of course, your knowledge of your particular market will be essential here - it may be that it's perfectly normal in your industry to have equipment service personnel on staff. (Even so, the posting indicates that they believe that they don't have enough people on the job – good knowledge to have.)

They may have documentation for their products, as well as online versions of their advertising materials. These can be invaluable resources for learning more about their offerings, particularly with an eye towards explaining to customers what makes your products or services superior.

In the past, you might have been able to lay hands on this sort of information by using expensive "mystery shoppers" or by making phone calls, posing as a customer yourself. However, it's very likely that you can now gather it from the comfort of your desk, without the expense or having to call on your drama coach to avoid being discovered.

3. Check local media

Before the advent of the Internet, you could find articles on a given business only by visiting the newspaper's morgue where they maintain a library of all of their back issues. In some cases, the indexes were excellent, maintained by professionals, and you could easily find the information you sought. However, you might also miss the most essential piece of data, simply for lack of the time to search all possibilities.

Now, you can usually visit the Web site of your local news media outlets and do a keyword search against years of articles. In a few cases, you'll be asked to pay for these searches. It may be worth your while to do so, depending on the importance of the article.

If you haven't previously visited the sites of your local media outlets, you'll probably find their Web sites listed in the masthead of print media and mentioned during news shows on broadcast media. Failing that, you can always do a search engine sweep to locate their sites.

Good search terms, of course, include the business name and the names of any principals you may have discovered along the way, as well as any prior business names that you may run across. You might also have a look for other businesses that may have previously existed in the same location. (Enter the address into your favorite search engine.) This may give you insight into the effectiveness of a given retail location, or even help you come across earlier businesses that the same people have run.

Don't overlook any local business journals in which your competitors may have been covered, and also don't forget to look in national media sources such as the Wall Street Journal. You never know when some small organization is going to garner the attention of major media, and there's often a *lot* of information uncovered in an article in one of these outlets.

4. Check local job listings

Every business runs on its people, and so anytime a competitor is going to make a major move, they'll almost inevitably telegraph the timing and nature of that move by opening up a bunch of positions. Those openings will often make it onto the Web, in one form or another.

Many very small businesses don't include job postings on their own Web sites. However, this doesn't mean that this valuable intelligence information is always unavailable. Look again at your local newspaper's Web site, to see if they have a section corresponding with their help-wanted ads. Look, too, at the large national job-hunting sites, such as www.monster.com, www. vault.com, hotjobs.yahoo.com or www.careerjournal.com. If your state employment agency posts listings online, you can sometimes glean information from these as well, although they do tend to withhold the names of the hiring organizations unless you're an applicant for one of the positions.

Job listings, even without a hiring company listed, can sometimes serve as an early-warning system. If you see a flurry of postings for people in your specialty, you may decide that it's a good time to give your employees a raise – just to keep them loyal. Too, you can be prepared for the arrival of a new player in your market.

5. Public notices

Many government agencies' regulations require that businesses publish public notice of planned activities. This information can sometimes be found on print media Web sites, as it's usually included in their classifieds sections. Typical listings from this resource will include land-use actions and licensing requests (particularly liquor and tobacco licenses).

More interesting, however, if you're in competition with a publicly held company, are the SEC filings. In order to give their stockholders the information needed to make decisions about buying and selling shares in a company, these filings require that your competitors lay open their balance sheet, discuss any risky plans that they intend to undertake, and review their most serious competitors. These filings are available both on the SEC's Web site (www.sec.gov/edgar.shtml), and at stock-tracking sites such as finance.yahoo.com and moneycentral.msn.com.

Obviously, this is a terrific set of information to have at your disposal. If they're making gobs of money, perhaps their prices are too high – or perhaps they've figured out how to do things more efficiently, and you can try to emulate them. If they're losing money, this gives you a chance to sow the seeds of doubt in your customers' minds.

The language that most organizations use in discussing future intentions is couched in legalistic disclaimers and dire warnings that things may not go as planned – it just begs to be quoted. Most interesting though, can be the review of *their* competition that most annual statements include. Here, you may get a chance to see how they see your company – again, this can be quotable stuff. Regardless, these filings are liable to be fascinating reading, and they'll likely give you tremendous insights into your competitors' businesses.

6. Newsgroup archives

At groups.google.com, you can find hundreds of millions of messages, representing online conversations about any topic under the sun. Newsgroups are such a rich resource that Project 18 in this book is devoted to their use – but the archives are a special case, and particularly relevant to online competitive research.

Search on your competitors' domain names, the name of the company, any proprietary product names, and the names of any personnel (current or past), and you'll quickly find every message they've ever posted on these discussion groups. While some of these will be irrelevant to developing business intelligence about your competitors (postings to hobby groups, for example), they may still give you a better idea of what sort of people you're up against.

If you're in a technical field, your competitors may have posted – or answered – questions; the nature of these questions can be very illuminating as to their technical expertise and direction. If there's been a controversy of some sort in your market, it's probably been discussed in the newsgroups, and your competitors may have joined in that discussion.

7. Pulling it all together

Now that you've conducted the raw research, it's useful to put the data into a standardized format so that you and your employees can refer to it easily. This format should include the most critical facts right up front – annual sales, number of employees, profitability and so forth. You may want to include a brief summary of the competitor's business practices and their position in the marketplace.

Any products or services that you offer in direct competition to theirs merit a discussion of relative strengths and weaknesses. This information can also give you ideas on improvements you can implement that will make you stronger in comparison to them. One format that's very effective for this sort of information is a comparison checklist, such as you often see in advertising. Indeed, once you've developed this grid for your internal uses, you may find it worthwhile to create a version of it for your customers' reference.

You should plan to spend a little time every month keeping these dossiers current – particularly in the Internet age, businesses change very quickly. In addition, you'll often find the greatest value in being able to integrate earlier intelligence with new information. Trends can reveal themselves very handily when you regularly go back and check the currency of a detailed competitive intelligence file.

Assessing Results

As you've learned more about how your competitors address the same challenges you face, you will have probably come up with many good ideas to leverage this information. Either they're doing things that you can learn from, or perhaps they're conducting business in ways that you'd like to bring to the attention of their customers who may be considering defecting. You may also gain information that you can use to encourage them to consider defecting.

In any event, competitive intelligence should give you results in those parts of your business where you're engaged in the most direct competition. Being able to train your sales force quickly and efficiently about what they're up against will increase their effectiveness. All of this will help to remove obstacles in your sales process, which should give you increased sales, as well as reduced sales cycle time and expense.

What's Next?

In the course of this project, you've probably seen a lot of things that you'd like to incorporate into your own Web site, which you can do in the course of Project 8, where you'll create a basic Web site. In addition, as you visited the archives of the Usenet newsgroups, you probably got a sense of how you can use these discussion groups. You'll learn more about newsgroups in Project 18.

Do set aside some time each month to review the information you've gathered and to revisit the conclusions you've drawn. Your sense of your place in the market – and your ability to positively influence that position – will improve along with the quality and completeness of this data.

Project 7:
Basic E-commerce

Web-enabled e-commerce is the ultimate goal for many organizations' Internet plans. For a small business, getting started can be surprisingly easy. With some of the services available to online entrepreneurs, you can have a storefront up and running in no time flat.

Prerequisites

You must have an Internet connection. Some of the steps in this project will also require that you have a listing of your inventory in an electronic format (see Project 22).

Cost projections

This project should cost under $100 per month, depending on the options you choose, and the volume of items you offer and sell online.

Goals

Starting to sell online offers many obvious business benefits. You will gain access to a new market, and nearly every sale you make online will be brand new business. Starting an e-commerce initiative is a substantial enough undertaking that it warrants developing a complete business plan. If successful, your profit and loss statement will be wildly different than it is now.

Procedures

1. Auction sites

Tens of thousands of people sell online every day, many of them for the first time. Online auction sites allow individuals – and businesses – to enter the world of e-commerce with a minimal investment of time, and with very controllable risks.

The undisputed market leader in this arena is eBay, although most every major portal site also has one form or another of auction. Some of the leaders are www.ebay.com, of course, as well as auctions.yahoo.com and auctions.amazon.com. Yahoo! has recently set themselves apart from the rest by going to a strictly advertising-supported model, charging no fees for listings.

There are also niche auction sites for everything from poultry eggs for hatching, to travel memorabilia. If what you have to sell fits into one of these niches, you may be able to avoid being overlooked in the hubbub of one of the larger, busier sites. If you choose one of the sites other than eBay, you will likely find that you're reaching fewer potential bidders, but they may be more determined to find a specialized item.

The basic premise of all of these sites, though, is that sellers list their items, together with a detailed description and even photographs, and buyers can then bid on the items, until the auction ends.

Unlike a physical auction, most online auctions end at a specific time, rather than when the last bidder has gone as high as he or she will go. Even so, some bidders will get caught up in the excitement, and end up bidding more than they might have spent if they had just purchased the item outright.

There are variations in capability at the different auction sites, but some of the major features include automatic proxy bidding, reserve prices, dutch auctions and instant purchases. Most auction sites also feature credit card payment systems, many of which you can use even without a merchant account.

An automatic proxy bid allows the buyer to make a bid for an item, and specify that he or she is willing to raise that bid to a given amount. The auction site will handle raising the bid, up to the maximum that the bidder has specified, by set increments. If two bidders both have proxies set up, the site will automatically play them off against each other until one of them has the high bid.

A reserve price allows you to set a minimum price that you'd like to get for an item, but not display that price. With most auction sites, where you are normally bound to complete the transaction regardless of the price your item draws, this gives you an out in the event that the final bid is no where near acceptable. On the other hand, it also allows you to start the bidding low – which can help to drive interest. Items that have a lot of bids are frequently featured in the listings, and most sites allow bidders to look for very active items.

A dutch auction is designed for those times when you have a quantity of identical items that you'd like to sell in multiple lots. Each buyer enters their bid, until all of the lots are spoken for, at some price. After that, until the end of the auction, any higher bids will simply knock the lowest bids off the list of successful buyers. Buyers can bid for any quantity; if their bid is successful, they will purchase the entire quantity they've bid on at the same price.

Sometimes you'd like to offer the buyer a chance to simply purchase an item outright, at a named price, without having to competitively bid and wait for the end of the auction. For these instances, most auction sites offer a "buy now" or "instant purchase" option. You would typically set the "buy now" price fairly near to the retail price. At some auction sites, the option disappears completely at the first bid, which can allow the price of the item to rise above what it might be worth in a normal sale – well to your benefit, as a seller.

You can try out e-commerce for yourself with just one item at auction. Pick something that you just want to be rid of – perhaps it's overstock, or a return. (If you sell returned merchandise at an online auction, it's proper to identify it as such.)

Decide what the minimum is you would accept for it, and set that as the starting bid for the auction. (A lower minimum bid may better ensure that the item attracts interest – but you may end up stuck selling it at a bargain-basement price.) Give a thorough and accurate description of the item, noting if it's new or used, in the original packaging, its condition and so on.

Spelling is important, as bidders will search on keywords, and a misspelled item name or description can keep most bidders from finding your item. Bargain hunters use misspellings to find items that haven't attracted much attention – great for them, but not so good for your bottom line.

If you have a digital camera, a photo of your item will help drive interest and assure bidders as to the condition of the item. Nearly all auction items include pictures these days, so an item with no picture will get far less attention than one with even a mediocre photo.

Determine how much you will need to charge for shipping, and list that in the description as well. You could simply state that the buyer will be responsible for actual shipping and handling, but a fixed shipping charge will give your potential bidders a better idea of what their total cost will be.

Some auction sites will also let you include a link for bidders to calculate actual shipping costs, based on your location and the weight and size of the item. This option may cost a little bit to include, but it will probably simplify the shipping question, both for you and for your potential bidders.

If you can accept payment via credit card, say so. You will have a number of options in this regard. Each of the auction sites offers credit card processing, with fairly standard merchants' terms and fees. You may be able to do better through your existing merchant account, but you'll need to come up with a secure way for the eventual buyer to communicate their card number to you.

Alternatively, you can use a service such as PayPal (www.paypal. com), which will permit you to accept credit cards with no particular hassle. The idea of this service is that people can send

44

you money via your email address. In practice, you should sign up with them in advance, and go through their account verification procedures. Once this is done, you will be able to move money from your online account to your bank checking account fairly conveniently, and at a minimal cost. (If you're running a large volume of transactions through their system, the charge are comparable to merchant-services agreements.)

Since PayPal was acquired by eBay, they've built in a lot of integration between their systems. This is great if you're using eBay, but not much help if you're using one of the other auction services. (This is probably a large part of the reason for the acquisition...)

You can usually set a time frame for the auction to last. It's probably to your advantage to keep it pretty short. Many bidders will sort the auction listings based upon how much longer the auctions will last, and items whose end dates are more than a few days out may initially be overlooked.

As the auction begins, you may be discouraged by an apparent lack of interest in your item. Don't be too concerned – many bidders wait until the last hour, or even the final minutes of an auction. Some more "predatory" bidders will even wait until the final seconds of an auction, in an attempt to prevent anyone else from outbidding them prior to the end.

During the course of the auction, potential buyers may contact you with questions. Depending on the site that you use, these questions and your answers may be visible to all. You should strive to be very responsive to auction questions – this will tend to influence your eventual ratings, which will impact your reputation in future auctions.

Once the auction ends, it's good practice to immediately contact your winning bidders to arrange payment and fulfillment. If you have set up a means to accept online credit card payments, you should ship the item as soon as you have confirmation of payment.

If you and the buyer have agreed to a money order or other verified funds check, you should ship once you have received the check or money order. With a personal check, it's normally acceptable to delay shipping until the check clears. Whatever your intention is, be sure to communicate it clearly to the buyer, and consider outlining your policy in the item listing.

Most of the auction sites charge a fee for you to list your items, and many of them also charge a percentage-based fee once the auction ends. They will also offer additional services, such as higher prominence on listings, at additional cost.

As you continue selling at auction, you may decide that you need to find a more efficient means of managing your auctions. To address this need, most of the sites will allow you to submit your items in bulk. Consult the instructions at the particular auction site for details.

2. Pre-built online shops

Whether you've dabbled in auction selling or have chosen to bypass that route entirely, at some point, you will probably want to explore the choices available to you for a regular Web store-front. Many of the same firms that have come to dominate online auctions also have credible offerings in this realm.

These services span the range from quite inexpensive – and inflex-ible – to moderately priced, and tremendously capable. Some the better options to compare are zshops.amazon.com, smallbusiness.yahoo.com/merchant, and stores.ebay.com. Each has its benefits and drawbacks.

Each offers the ability to keep your inventory current through a bulk uploading service. They all offer the capability to accept credit cards, although with some you must establish a merchant account or link your existing merchant account into their site. You may be able to make the storefront look just as if it were part of your site.

With some providers, you will be required to keep your inven-tory levels up-to-date. Some even offer the ability to manage all of your inventory tracking right online. This can be a very convenient option, particularly since it will probably enable you to manage your inventory from any computer with an Internet connection.

3. Shipping and handling fees

If you've never done mail order retailing before, you may be surprised at how much shipping can cost. In addition, you may find that your customers are highly resistant to paying the actual costs of shipping, plus your added costs to package and prepare their order.

Different online retailers have tried different tactics. Some attempt complete openness – they charge a fixed handling fee for the packaging and so forth, and then charge the actual shipping costs. Unless your prices are significantly lower than the competition's, though, you're probably already figuring in some overhead costs – and the customers are very aware of this fact. They often balk at this approach to shipping.

If the site doesn't handle the calculations, figuring exact shipping can also mean either multiple contacts to the customer to determine where they're located, and then to communicate to them what the actual total for their order is. In many cases, an online shopper will simply leave your site if they can't see the total charge, including shipping, before they commit to the order.

Other merchants charge a flat shipping rate for a given item, averaging out the geographic differentials, and building in a portion for average handling costs. This is a fairly well accepted method, and it does let the customer see a grand total cost for the item right up front. On the other hand, it also requires a fairly extensive amount of administration, particularly as shipping rates change, or if your geographic market assumptions are off.

Still other merchants regard shipping charges as an opportunity to "make up" the discounts that their posted prices reflect. If your basic prices are very heavily discounted, and the total cost including shipping and handling is still lower than the competition's, you may not loose too many customers with this approach. However, many online consumers will be irate at what they perceive as a "bait and switch" pricing policy, which could impact your reputation.

Finally, some online sellers simply incorporate the shipping and handling charge into the price of the item, clearly state that there are no hidden charges, and trust the consumer to be able to discern the advantage of a clearly posted total price.

In part, the choice that you make here should be driven by what the norms are in your market. If you are selling to consumers who are accustomed to seeing shipping fees that comprise a significant portion of their overall cost, you can either follow suit – or make a big deal over offering a clear advantage.

If you rarely or never see shipping and handling mentioned on your competitors' sites, and the prices appear to be slightly inflated over normal cost plus margin, you can probably guess what's accepted practice. Again you can either go along, or try to lure customers with low prices, hoping that they'll stick with you through the addition of the shipping charges.

Whatever policy you choose to follow, you will probably want to do what's possible to minimize the costs – whether they're your direct costs, or passed through to customers. As your shipping volume picks up, you will qualify for discounts and special rates from the various shippers. In addition, you may be able to get access to preferential rates by signing long-term agreements with one firm or another.

If your products may be subject to shipping restrictions, be sure that you clearly state that in your online materials. Food, drink, plant material, and many more items may be banned from shipping into certain jurisdictions, and your shipping companies may have further restrictions. Be sure that you investigate what the limitations may be before you ship an item, as the legal or contractual liabilities may fall on you rather than the recipient.

When you sell items that may be given as gifts, you should offer the option to exclude the charges from any invoice that you pack in the shipment. If you offer gift-wrapping, be sure that you don't then include an invoice on top of everything that details what's hidden within the colorful paper, as that may defeat the purpose.

Be sure to always clearly label who a package is for, and exactly where it's shipped from. Include your phone number and Web site on the label, so that the recipient can allay any suspicions without having to open the package. In order to make a good impression, it's also a good idea to always use new packaging, and of course, pack items securely and appropriately.

4. Taxes

Like most mail order, the current state of understanding about retail sales taxes is that you need not collect sales tax on items sold out of state. As of this writing, this understanding is embodied by a U.S. Supreme Court ruling. This Supreme Court ruling also prevents the states from imposing double taxation on e-commerce, so your customers won't be forced to pay sales taxes in your state *and* their own.

Items sold to customers in your state (or any in which you have a substantial business presence) are usually subject to sales tax, . The current Internet tax moratorium bars state sales or usage taxes on Internet access services, but not products sold over the Internet.

However, the field is constantly changing, and the various levels of government clearly see Internet commerce as a tempting target for their ever-growing revenue requirements. You should sit down with your accountant or lawyer to determine what the current state of e-commerce taxation is in your jurisdiction.

5. Maintaining your reputation

More than ever, on the Internet your reputation is key to your success. In the bricks-and-mortar world, if a customer feels that he or she has been treated badly, he may tell a few friends. An Internet-savvy customer who feels abused can tell a few thousand friends.

Most of the auction sites, as well as many of the basic hosted e-commerce sites have a highly formalized means of quantifying your reputation, through the use of feedback forums. Every buyer – and every seller – is encouraged to leave feedback on each transaction. Positive or negative, the feedback is averaged out, and a score is derived. These feedback scores are often included in every item listing, and buyers do pay attention to them.

If you have a customer with whom you are unable to reach a satisfactory resolution to a problem, and you get a negative rating on an item, you will usually be given a chance to respond to the feedback. Do so calmly, laying out any facts that you can, and then move on. Regard it as a learning opportunity, and be sure that you don't repeat any mistakes that may have lead to the misunderstanding in the first place.

A strong reputation can also be to your distinct advantage. That same customer who tells thousands of people about his or her poor experience with you can use the same means to talk about a positive experience. As in any form of business, referrals are to be treasured – all the more so when they put your name in front of a worldwide audience.

Assessing Results

You should notice many changes to your business in the course of completing this project. Sales volume should have risen; costs may have dropped. The geographic distribution of your market will likely have changed wildly.

What's Next?

Now that you've tried out e-commerce, you can consider moving your storefront onto your own site. Project 8 will guide you through creating a Web site, and Project 23 describes some more advanced e-commerce methods that you can employ.

Project 8:
Building a Basic Web Site

One of the biggest steps you can take in opening the door to the use of the Internet in your small business is to establish your own Web site. Unfortunately, it's also where many small businesses make their biggest online mistakes. Review the Rookie Mistakes, below, before you proceed – with any luck, you can avoid making some of these errors.

Rookie Mistakes

"Panacea" Theory

A great Web site cannot solve flaws in your basic business model. The "dot-bust" has given us an ample proof of this – business plans that sounded squirrelly in the offline world were not suddenly transformed into sheer genius by slapping an "e" on the front or a "dot-com" on the back. If you're inadequately serving your existing market, increasing the size of that market through the use of the Internet's just going to compound your troubles, not solve them.

"Free" Web Site

There are a fair number of offers out there for a free or low-cost "point of presence" Web site. There are also a fair number of reasons to avoid this option. Primarily, you do get what you pay for here. A free site will be nothing more than a Web page or two where someone has slapped some text from one of your brochures or from an email to the site builder into a pre-made template. You've probably seen sites like these – and you probably remember how uninspiring they were.

It's important that your site change from time to time too, or else it becomes what's known as a "cobweb" site. Few of these offers give you a way to maintain your site and give it the timely call to action it needs.

Flaming Logos

Some years ago, IBM ran a television ad depicting a couple of gonzo Web designers demonstrating a version of a Web site for a client, on which they had made it appear that the client's logo was on fire. The message of the ad was absolutely on point – glitz for the point of glitz is pointless to your customers. Some Web design folks haven't yet figured this out, and it's hard to even call this a rookie mistake. A lot of organizations that should really know better commit this error a lot of the time. Don't be one of them.

Prerequisites

You will need access to a computer with an Internet connection. Ideally, this should be at your place of business. Your current marketing materials and any market research you have into your customer base will also be useful.

Cost projections

You'll spend between $10 and $50 per year and an hour or so of your time for your domain name registration. You should budget from $15 to $500 annually for Web hosting services, depending upon your requirements.

Plan to spend $1,000 to $25,000 (depending upon the complexity of your needs) for Web design and site creation services OR 4-plus weeks' worth of study time and another 4 to 6 weeks' time to create the site yourself. Hiring someone to do the first version for you is usually a very good investment, unless you have previous experience and/or a knack for graphic design as well as coding.

Add $25 to $500 per month for site maintenance OR 4 to 20 hours per month of your own time. Again, it's probably a worthwhile investment to hire an expert, at least in the beginning. Asking your Web designer to show you what he or she is doing, so that you can eventually take over is usually accepted well by professionals.

Goals

A Web site will move many of the same business metrics as any other sort of advertising effort. Lead volume, lead quality, sales volume, and sales cycle time can all be improved through a good Web site.

In addition, if you provide post-sales support to your customers, you can raise the efficiency of that support very easily. We'll cover in Project 21 how to improve your customer support dramatically by using the Web, but there's a lot you can do without the more advanced steps described there. This can impact your returned-goods, repeat customer and referral measurements.

Procedures

1. Register your domain name

While you can skip this step, your Web site will look a lot more professional with your own business name as the address, rather than "users.aol.com/biffdinger/mybusiness.html." Think of it as your street address on the Internet. Given how little it costs, this is a very worthwhile exercise.

Start by going to a domain registration service – www.godaddy.com, www.register.com and www.internic.com are a few of the leading players in this market. Your own ISP may also offer this service, sometimes at a discount over the standard rate of $10-50 per year per domain name. Many Web hosts will likewise have this service available, and may include it for free when you use their hosting services.

One of the frustrations you may encounter in trying to register a domain is that a lot of the good names are already taken. For example, if your business is named "Smiths Furniture," you will likely find that smithsfurniture.com is already taken. However, smithsfurniturestore.com, smithsfurnitureco.com or smiths-furniture.com may be available. You may have to do quite a bit of experimentation before you find a suitable domain name.

Remember, though, that your customers will have to type in this domain name whenever they want to visit your Web site – so it should be relatively short, easy to remember, and closely associated with your business name. So if you've been doing business as Smith's Furniture, "smithcofinefurniturestoreinc.com" might not be the best domain name to settle upon.

This problem has been somewhat alleviated by the addition of several new "top level domains" (TLDs) – in other words, in place of the .com, you'll can choose from .biz, .store, and others. However, the current experience of holders of .net and .org domains tends to indicate that the majority of the Web surfing audience out there anticipates a .com at the end of nearly any domain. It's similar to the real-world experience of businesses located just off Main Street – their competitors on the main drag are somewhat more likely to draw the casual shopper. Some of the alternate TLDs are more expensive to secure than .com and the like; some are less expensive.

Be aware that there is a brisk business in simply registering every domain name that might be of use to someone someday, and then offering to sell these registrations at inflated prices. While this can be a legitimate activity, there are also very strict rules that may allow you to challenge the right of someone to register a domain name that is clearly associated with your business name. However, the process of fighting a domain-ownership challenge can be very costly and time-consuming – which is how these so-called "cybersquatters" stay in business. It may be worth a few dollars to buy the rights to the perfect domain name, rather than settling for something really unreasonable or battling it out for years.

2. Choose your content

After having done Project 6, where one of your most valuable information sources was your competitors' own Web sites, you may be feeling a little paranoid about what you're going to include on your site. The guidelines to keep in mind are, "Can my competitors get their hands on this information relatively easily already?" and, "Will its availability to my customers be of great enough benefit to outweigh the risk of my competitors having free access to it?"

In most cases, unless we're talking about industrial secrets, the benefits will outweigh the risks in the long run – particularly when you consider how few businesses conduct a formal competitive intelligence process such as you established in Project 6.

The guiding principle as to what you should include on your Web site must be how you'd like your customers and prospects to see you. If you have information that's going to convince them, on the spot, that you're the best possible supplier for their needs, by all means include that. If you have material that's completely unrelated to your company's business (personal photos, online games, miscellaneous downloads and the like will usually fall into this category), leave it out.

It's extremely important to be very careful about including any sort of material that may be copyrighted by someone else. If you're found with someone else's intellectual property on your site, the consequences can be grave. At the very least, you will be asked to remove it at once, and you may be sued or even prosecuted in some jurisdictions. If you don't own the content, or have explicit permission to use it on the Web, don't put it on your site.

3. Think about Web design

If you haven't yet done a lot of surfing the Web, now's a really good time to do so. Take note of what sites you find the easiest to use, and why. Notice the features in product information, customer contact pages, ordering processes and so forth that work for you – and those that confuse you or slow you down. You don't have to become a Web design guru – but the time you spend now will probably save you hours of argument and frustration with your Web designer later.

There are a number of excellent books on the market about Web usability – one of the best is *Don't Make Me Think*, by Steve Krug. It's well worth your time, whether you plan to hire an outside consultant or you are considering taking on the task yourself, to get this book from your local library. (You will probably find that you want to buy a copy to keep for reference, but that's your option.)

One final thing to keep in mind as you work on your site design is the ADA (Americans with Disabilities Act). Some have interpreted this law to require that Web sites be designed for accessibility to visually impaired or otherwise disabled visitors. In general, this means that images should always be described with alternate text, and fancy multimedia components should be avoided if possible. Consider using a plain sans serif font (such as "Arial") to make reading your content easier for dyslexics.

4. Decide who will create the site

Many small businesses have not yet focused on the Internet because they're too busy taking care of the customers standing in front of them. There's nothing wrong with this! Once you have made the decision to use the Internet, though, it's time to take a long, honest look in the mirror. If you're going to need outside help, now is the time to figure that out.

Deciding whether to do the work within your organization or to hire someone to do it for you is a significant choice. Perhaps your organization is blessed with an individual who's been studying how to leverage the Internet for years. If your in-house Internet guru has launched a dozen prior organizations onto the Web, you can be pretty well assured that she can get yours out there, too.

If your organization's first experience with the Internet was Project 1 in this book, you may feel pretty confident that it will be worth your while to bring someone in to do the work for you. Indeed, most small businesses don't have a lot of people sitting around, looking for something to do, and so finding the time from anyone on staff already may be impossible.

For most small businesses though, the answer's not so clear. You may feel that you can pick up the necessary technical skills yourself. Don't forget, though, that your time has value, and it would be a mistake to spend so much time intensively studying the necessary disciplines that you neglect your business.

If you do decide to look outside of your organization, ask to see a prior portfolio of client work from anyone you consider. Your neighbor's high-school-aged cousin may not be the best choice for the job – or perhaps she is. A portfolio will help you to make that determination. Have a close look at the sites they've designed. Can you quickly find what you're looking for? Are they attractive and up-to-date? Are the technologies employed appropriate and unobtrusive?

You should also ask to speak with their prior clients in order to get an idea of how easy - or difficult - it is to work with them. Some people in the field are utterly brilliant at the technical underpinnings, but will get prickly and defensive when their design choices are questioned. You'll be a lot more successful if you can find someone who's glad to explain each choice to you, with the intention of educating you. And of course, they should be open to your reasonable suggestions. After all, you are their customer.

Generally speaking however, the person you select to do the work – internally or externally – should have a firm grounding in Web usability and design, a solid knowledge of the technical building blocks of the Web, and a good sense of marketing, particularly in your specific market space. If you can avoid someone who's enamored of splashy graphics and neat techno-wizardry for its own sake, you will do better at avoiding the "flaming logo" rookie mistake.

5. Finalize design choices

You should probably ask your Web designer to supply at least a couple of different designs for you to consider. Ask for a typical front page, a second-level navigation page, and a detail page for each design you will weigh. You should also give the designer some general guidelines as to what you expect. Again, knowledge of your typical customer – or at least the typical customer you expect to visit your Web site – will be very useful information to your Web designer.

One critical piece of information that any good designer will require from you is some idea of the sort of technology your customer base uses. If you're serving technically savvy people, the designer is a lot less constrained than if your customer base is more likely to have older computers and slower Internet connections. When in doubt, err to the side of simplicity – after all, a Web site that displays quickly on a slow modem and old computer will display even more quickly on more advanced systems.

When you're considering the front-page designs, there are a couple of things to look for. First of all, is it very clear what your company does? Can you see where you would find out how to contact your company, via phone, email or (if applicable) fax or walk-in? Can you see where you'd click to find out more about your products or services, or even (potentially) to buy them? If you serve multiple audiences, is it clear to each of them where they can find information specific to their needs? Finally, does the design convey the necessary information, while considering any constraints (technological or otherwise) that your customer base may have?

The second-level navigation page will usually be focused around a specific constituency among your customers, or a natural product-line grouping. Many of the same criteria apply on these pages as on the home page. Can you see clearly how to drill down to more detailed information? Is it obvious how you would return to the home page? Can you navigate easily to other major sections on the Web site, particularly any related second-level navigation pages?

Finally, in assessing a detail page, you want to again see the ability to easily return home. (Ideally, this will be identical throughout the site – with the possible exception of the home page itself.) You also want to be able to quickly return to the level of navigation you just left – without having to resort to the back arrow in your browser. Bear in mind, though, that most users will naturally use the back button heavily as they navigate your site – so your design should be friendly to this navigational method, too.

For all of the pages, you want to see a reasonable amount of information given. In newspapers, the space "above the fold" – that is, visible when the paper's on the newsstand before you pick it up – is coveted most highly. On the Web, the analogous concept is the top of the page. The top of your page – the portion visible in your typical visitor's browser window without scrolling – is where you'll keep or lose someone casually surfing through your site.

If possible, you'd like to avoid forcing the user to scroll down for essential information. You nearly always want to avoid forcing them to scroll left-to-right. Recall that the modern "wheel mouse" allows you to quickly perform vertical scrolling – but horizontal requires that your visitors take their eyes off of the content to manipulate their browser window controls. (The newest generation of "wheel mice" address this by adding a tilt control to the wheel for horizontal scrolling – but these are still relatively rare, and you should not base your design choices on the assumption that such a technology will gain instant customer acceptance.)

Finally and most critically, will the proposed design attract your customers or repel them? You probably know your audience better than anyone, but this is not a bad time to talk to a few trusted customers, and ask their opinions. You can even show them the designs on paper and just ask them the same questions that you asked yourself in this step. The answers may support your own conclusions or refute them entirely. Either way, they will be very interesting to hear – so you should listen with an open mind.

6. Build the site

Once you've made the large design decisions, the work of actually creating the site becomes almost anticlimactic. Some content will have special requirements, of course, but by and large your content creation can simply be a matter of putting the content you've selected into the form you've selected.

When you have a working model of the site available to you, spend some time with it. This would be another good time to bring in several trusted customers. Many usability experts even bring in people off the street to review a design. If someone completely unfamiliar with your business can answer the questions posed above, then the site design is probably going to be a success.

7. Make hosting decisions

Now that you have the site complete, you need to figure out where to put it so that your customers and prospects can see it on the public Internet. There are a lot of options here – everything from sites that will host for free to very low-cost, to full-blown Cadillac solutions, which are likely more than you need at this stage.

Most businesses today chose to have their Web site content hosted on a service provider's computer at their facility. Your ISP may offer this service as part of your Internet service package; discuss with your Web designer whether it meets your site's needs.

The free hosting options (including www.freeservers.com, tripod. lycos.com, and geocities.yahoo.com) typically insert banners and other advertising into your pages, which you will have little or no control over.

Many of these same firms – as well as any number of other providers – will offer a similar bare-bones hosting service at low cost, without their banner ads. This is probably the most appropriate choice for a small business just trying to set up their first Web site. Other providers to consider in this space include www.hostfora-dollar.com, www.netfirms.com and smallbusiness.yahoo.com.

Be sure that you can use your hard-won domain name with any of these that you consider. Most places that offer to host your content on their systems will have clear instructions as to how to move your content up to their computers, as well as how to point your Web address at it. In any event, you can probably ask your Web designer to take care of this final task as part of the job.

There are other options for hosting your site, but they're unlikely to be appropriate to a small business. These include locating a server at the ISP's facility (sometimes referred to as "colocation"), or serving up your Web site on a machine at your own location. Both of these require pretty extensive infrastructure and are increasingly rare choices, as the options offered by ISPs become richer and more compelling.

8. Go live!

When the final bug is squashed and the last page is checked in, and it's time to make your site live, it's a tremendous feeling. Of course, the first email you'll probably get will be someone (either on your team or outside of the company) who's noticed a grammar error. Little things like that you will fix immediately, and the site will improve dramatically in its first week online. Larger opportunities for improvement will also present themselves. It's all part of the process, so don't worry too much about it.

The next time you place an order for stationery or business cards, be sure that your Web address is now included on them. Start telling your customers that they can find you on the Web. If you have a retail store, consider putting your URL on your door, right under your hours – then a disappointed would-be walk-in customer may suddenly become a satisfied online customer.

9. Mid-course adjustments

You're bound to find things that can be improved, as you review the customer feedback and results measurements. Making small corrections as you go is perfectly fine – just be sure that you continue to keep an eye on the measures of success, and that you can undo any changes that don't appear to be working.

10. Change is constant

Budget some time every month – or every week – to review the content on your Web site and see if there's something that should be updated, added or removed, as your business and marketplace evolves. You may find that the changes needed are easy enough that you can take over the maintenance of your site within your organization. Or, you may decide to retain your Web designer to keep things current.

Regardless of who actually does the work, it's critical that it be done. By this time, you've probably come across sites that looked like they'd be interesting, but which are so hopelessly out of date that they are completely useless to you as a customer, and so you moved on. Specials that have expired months ago, "news" that's old, and outmoded site designs all cause visitors to look elsewhere for their solutions. You need to ensure that your business isn't being represented by such a "cobweb" site to avoid having your customers do the same.

As your site evolves, be sure that all of the links on it still work. It's embarrassing to get an email from a big customer, telling you about a broken link. It's especially important to regularly check links to external sites. You may have advance warning of changes on your own site, but you're unlikely to have any notice of changes at others.

Unless the overall design is actively detracting from the usefulness of your site, try to resist the urge to do frequent makeovers. Just like any other major investment, you need to weigh whether or not the expense will give you a reasonable return on investment. You probably don't remodel your office every six months, or even every couple of years – so why would you do that to your online presence?

Even given the concept of "Internet time," a solid site design can remain current for many years. Many leading sites leave their basic site design alone for a very long time, only making changes with extreme caution. Your repeat visitors will not benefit from a jarring change every time they stop by – and neither will your business.

Assessing Results

You can start to gauge the value of your Web site to your business by looking at the number of leads that you get from it. Are they more likely to buy than prospects who come to you through traditional channels? Do they place orders more quickly, resulting in a shortened sales cycle? Do they buy more, driving top-line revenue?

The return on investment of your Web site will vary depending upon the nature of your business, but the long-term returns will be almost inevitable. For some businesses, the first order that comes directly from their online efforts pays for the entire project. For others, success is slower to build. Regardless, your business has taken an important step forward by joining the Internet revolution in a visible way.

What's Next?

Now that you have a basic Web site, you can suddenly start to consider many of the other projects in this book. Project 9 will show you how to drive traffic to your site through some basic site-promotion activities. In Project 11, you'll learn how to follow the trails that your customers leave as they visit the site, which can help guide improvements to it.

Almost all of the remaining projects have as a prerequisite that you have a Web site – so now the real opportunities to enhance your business with this book are open to you. Congratulations!

Project 9:
Helping Them Find Your Site

"If you build it, they will come" does not necessarily apply on the Web. It's necessary to inform prospects and customers that you have a site, and to make it possible for casual browsers to find it. Fortunately, there are a lot of opportunities to promote Web sites.

Some means of driving traffic to your site are very low-cost, both in time and resources, and others, if the return justifies it, can involve spending some money. This project will focus on the low-cost approaches – later projects will guide you through some of the more advanced (and costly) ways to get the word out.

Prerequisites

You must have an active Web site, and access to a computer with an Internet connection. If you haven't already learned how to use search engines, this project will teach you more about them than you may ever have wanted to know.

In order to have an accurate measurement of the effectiveness of this project, you may want to simultaneously undertake Project 11 for traffic analysis.

Cost projections

Plan for approximately two hours to assess your current place-ment on search engines. If your Web site needs adjustments, you'll need to budget some time to complete those, or some money to have your site designer do it. In the beginning, you will probably want to spend an hour every week or two to monitor how your site is progressing on the search engines.

If you decide to re-print stationery or business cards to include your URL, be sure to budget for that as part of your site-promotion expenses. Plan for any fees for Yellow Pages listing changes, or to add online listings.

Goals

The primary thing that you'll see change as a result of this project is the number of visitors to your Web site. Of course, the more people who see your site, the more the objectives you set in Project 8 will be realized, so many of the same business metrics that applied there, will apply here.

Procedures

1. Get the word out

As mentioned in Project 8, as you get your Web site up and running, let your current customers know that they can now reach you via the Web. If you've been talking to customers via email, you should make sure to drop a note to each correspondent, letting them know that you're online.

Be sure to include your URL on any advertising materials that you create henceforth, as well as on your stationery and business cards. Post it on your door and include it in your answering machine or voicemail outbound message.

If you have signage at your location, be sure that your Web address is listed on that, as well as on any labeled company vehicles. You'll be surprised at how many people will see your URL as they're driving and make a note of it – particularly if you were able to secure a good domain name. If they had been thinking about purchasing a product or service that you provide, seeing a Web site named may just spur them to come check you out – and to go on to become a customer.

Add your URL to your Yellow Pages listing and be sure to include it in any online listing that you may get packaged with that advertising. Consider upgrading to an online listing, even if it costs extra. In many connected households, the paper Yellow Pages are hardly ever used – prospects go to their online versions first.

Finally, be sure to include your URL in your email signature. In most email packages, the software can automatically include a signature at the bottom of every message for you, so you don't have to type it every time. If you haven't used this feature already, you can learn more about it by consulting the documentation or online help for your particular software.

2. Understanding search engines

Internet search engines are your friends. Really. Over the long run, you'll probably see more traffic come in from the search engines than from any other source.

As you get started in trying to get your site and your content to show up on them though, you may catch yourself feeling that they are arbitrary, capricious and malicious in the way that they insist on missing your site. In most cases, they're not – but they do operate under a pretty well established set of rules.

There are a couple of major approaches to helping people find what they're after among the trillions of pages on the Internet. Most of the search engines use some combination of approaches to enable users to find the pages they want, without having to wade through hundreds of pages they're not interested in.

Keyword matches will bring up your site when the user enters a search term that either matches or is related to some text on your pages. So a user searching for "shoes" will find pages that contain the words shoe, shoes, boot, boots, sneakers, and so forth. Some of the more sophisticated implementations of this approach will extend it to conceptual matching – so that same search will now also include pages that discuss footwear in general.

In order to increase the relevance of the pages presented first, search engines may weigh a number of factors. These may include the number of times that a user with a similar search clicked on a given result, to how many pages throughout the Internet link to a specific result page, to how many times the keywords or key concepts appear on a given result page.

All of these methods are kept very close to the vest, for a number of reasons. Not only do the search engine firms have an interest in preventing their competitors from duplicating their systems, but they also want to keep Web sites from fooling their systems into returning irrelevant information. Indeed, some search engine companies even have policies that banish sites that attempt to "spoof" them into including irrelevant pages in their users' search results.

There are many articles on the Web on the topic of how search engines work and how to make them work in your favor. If you want more in-depth information than is included in this project, you can visit www.searchenginewatch.com, which is one of the leading authorities on the care and feeding of these services. Or do a search, on search terms such as "search engine algorithms," or "search engine technology."

One thing that you should probably *not* do is to use one of the services that "guarantee" top placement on search engines. While there are services that can manage your site submission tasks, it's difficult to separate the legitimate ones from the frauds – particularly as the results from either may be indistinguishable. Better to spend the money on improving your site content so that it accurately describes your products or services. In the long run, that is the true secret to being found via search engines.

All of this being said, please don't regard search engine placement as the be-all and end-all of your site's success. There are a lot of other ways for people to find your site and many of them will deliver higher-quality traffic – people more likely to buy – than even the best search engine.

Too, as you've probably noticed in your own usage of search engine results, users tend to skip past irrelevant results when they're looking for something specific. So even if, for example four highly-technical academic research papers keep getting higher placement in a test search you're spot-checking, remember that your customers will keep going until they find your listing.

3. Basic searches

Visit a couple of your favorite search engines, and do a quick search for your business name. Odds are if you've just launched your site, it won't even show up. However, if you're doing this project with a site that's been live for at least a couple of months, you may well find yourself near the top of the listings, if not at the top.

If your site didn't show up at all, go ahead and submit it – there will usually be some means of doing so somewhere on the site. At Google, you can visit www.google.com/webmasters/ for site-submission links. For Yahoo!, go to submit.search.yahoo. com/free/request. Ask Jeeves, Google and Yahoo! all maintain human-edited directories, so you'll need to follow their guidelines to submit your site for inclusion in these listings.

If your site did show up but did not appear at the top of the listings, there are a number of potential causes. If the problem is that your business name is not unique, try to think about how your customers and prospects might search for you. What sets your "Jones & Co. Hats" apart from all the other haberdasheries founded by Joneses? If you include the name of your town, does your Web site now show up nearer the top of the listings?

It may be, too, that one of the other measurements of relevancy mentioned earlier is causing your site to score lower – and there-fore show up lower – in the search. If this is the case, you can take steps to correct most of the deficiencies that the search engines may be seeing in your pages. Read up on what the search engine in question uses to rank results to understand what these steps are.

4. Searching by keyword

For this step, you'll need to continue to think like your custom-ers. If you've started Project 11 to analyze your Web site logs, you can actually see the keywords that they *have* been finding you through. Search on these same keywords to see where your site places in the results. Do a search for some key words that describe your products or services. Start with broad terms, and narrow it down to include specific brand names that you carry or specific services you provide.

If you have exclusive brands, you'll probably find that your results for this sort of search are pretty good. Otherwise your placement may not be so good – or your site may not show up at all. Again, try to think like a prospective customer – what sets your organization apart, what might they be looking for that your company provides better than anyone else – and what keywords might a customer use to look for those qualities?

Now that you have an idea of how well your site shows up in keyword searches, there are a couple of things that you can do very easily to increase the relevance of your site. First of all is the concept of "meta keywords." These are simply some hidden text on your page that gives an explicit list of keywords that pertain to your site. They'll commonly include any keywords that might not be included in the text content of your page. Some people even include competing company and brand names, although the ethics of this practice are debatable.

Don't expect meta-tag keywords to compensate for inadequate content. Despite what some people may claim, meta tags are not a magic bullet or a panacea. Nothing beats well-crafted textual content that's relevant to the needs of your visitors for ensuring good placement in search engine results.

5. Pay for placement

Some of the search engines have tried a formalized method of ensuring that your site is highly ranked on users' searches, where you pay for that privilege. If you have a site that will eventually score well in searches due to a good quantity of relevant content, simple patience will probably yield the same results. As an existing small business, it's unlikely that the month or two you gain will be a good investment.

However, if you want to make sure that your site is found, you can spend a few hundred dollars at this game and get the top billing that you seek. Note, though, that businesses that depend on the success of this ploy to make their site pay for itself are likely to be overestimating the potential for their Web site to make an immediate and substantive difference in their revenue mix.

6. Keyword Advertising

Most search engines offer another means of ensuring that your site is presented to customers who search on particular terms. You may have seen the "featured listings" or "sponsored link" listings that appear above or to the side of your search results.

In most cases, these are offered on a pay-per-click or pay-per-impression basis. (See Project 16 for more details about what these billing models mean.) They can offer a very economical means of ensuring the people who search for one of your brand names, or for your company name see your listing.

However, there are a few caveats. If the search term you want to use is too specific, it won't be used very often – and therefore, it may not be worth the search engine company's time to manage such a low-volume medium for you. If you choose a term that is already heavily advertised on, your listing may get lost in the din of other sponsored listings.

However, if you think that you can devise search terms that will navigate between these hazards, this can be an excellent way to grab the attention of people who are looking for your products or services. The two leading providers in this field are www.google. com and www.overture.com. Google, of course, presents the ads on their own site, as well as on those sites where they provide search engine services. Google's AdWords program embeds text-based ads into thousands of sites throughout the Internet, ranging from personal blogs to top-quality content sites. Overture serves a number of sites, including many of the leading portals. Check with the Web sites listed to learn who their current partners are.

7. Links

The unique power of the Web, beyond its ability to instantly communicate detailed information around the globe, is that it's designed to allow that information to be easily linked together. You can harness this aspect of the Web's capabilities fairly easily with just a little bit of work. In addition, this step will help your placement in many search engine results.

Start by looking at the Web sites of any local business associations that you belong to. Your Chamber of Commerce, credit union or community service organizations may all have Web sites that include links to their members' sites. In addition, if you are a member of a trade association specific to your market, they, too, may have Web listings for their members.

Consider contacting your suppliers to see whether they might be interested in swapping a link to your site for one to theirs. Even better, speak to your best customers about including you on their sites as well. Whether a business Web site or a personal site, a link from a satisfied customer is almost as good as a word-of-mouth referral – and sometimes better!

Assessing Results

If you've been successful in driving traffic to your site, you should see an increase in the overall traffic that it bears. You may also see changes in the quality of the visitors you get – it may improve, if your efforts were well targeted, or it may decline if they were too broad. You will probably notice that you spend more time answering emailed inquiries as traffic rises.

It's worth remembering that for most businesses, raw Web site traffic should *not* be considered to be a key business metric. Don't overlook the basics of good business management in order to focus too heavily on the amount of traffic your Web site receives. The Web is a means to influencing your business results – it's not usually a primary business objective.

What's Next?

In order to really understand where your visitors are coming from, you need to be able to analyze your Web site traffic. Project 11 will help you through that process, including determining where your *best* visitors are coming from, so that you can better focus your ongoing site promotion efforts.

More active means of bringing your online presence to the attention of your target audience are covered in Project 16, which discusses the use of banner advertising, and Project 17, which delves into other avenues for advertising online.

As you've spent more time online in the course of the last several projects, you may have come to the conclusion that you need a faster connection to the Internet. You may also have found that you'd like to reconsider the hosting decisions that you made in Project 8. In any case, Project 12 will guide you through some of the more popular options for moving beyond a dialup connection to the Internet.

Project 10:
Recruiting Online

Many small businesses use the Web to attract candidates for open positions. More job seekers than ever are turning first to the Internet to look for their next position. If they even look at traditional newspaper listings, it's just as likely to be on the newspaper's Web site. By implementing this project, you can start to attract the most qualified (and net-savvy!) candidates you've ever seen.

Prerequisites

You must have at least an email account; your own Web site is required if you want to post your openings under your full control.

Cost projections

In order to set your Web site up to display job postings, you will need to spend between 10 and 40 hours of your time, or budget around $300 to $2,000 to have a consultant do it. After that, figure on spending an hour or two for each position, converting it into HTML to post on your site.

In addition, the nationwide job-hunting sites charge a fee for their assistance in your recruiting efforts, so you should budget between $50 and $300 for each position, if you're planning to use these sites. Your local newspaper also probably offers online listings, and may represent a more affordable alternative.

Though these may seem like high costs, some studies have suggested that recruiting online is far less expensive than traditional means. Bear in mind, too, that an empty seat can be a gaping hole in your organization, and Internet recruiting has the potential to be much faster than older methods.

Goals

When you're hiring, you're interested in finding the best person you can afford for the job, at the lowest possible recruiting cost, and with the longest possible retention with your company. Using the Internet to recruit can help you accomplish all of these.

Procedures

1. Posting on your own site

Often, job seekers will select companies they'd like to work for, and then check to see what opportunities might exist with their target organizations. You should have a link from your home page (or possibly from your company information page) to a list of open positions. By convention, this link should be labeled either "Jobs" or "Careers" – the latter cultivates the thought that working for you can be a long-term opportunity.

Just as in any other venue, the listing should clearly lay out what specific job responsibilities the candidate will be expected to take on, what expectations you have about experience, skills, and education and any specific certifications or other criteria you may have. Specify what's required, as opposed to desired.

With each job, you should have a link to encourage the job seeker to apply on the spot. This can be as simple as a link to an email address, together with a description of what you would like to see from them – resume, curriculum vitae, portfolio, etc. After you've gone through Project 14, you may want to apply what you've learned there to creating an online form to gather the exact information you want.

You may have concerns about the wisdom of posting your open positions on the Web. After all, Project 6 in this very book discusses what a great source of competitive intelligence such postings can be. In this case, and at other points where you have to make a decision about posting potentially sensitive content on your Web site, consider the cost versus benefit question.

Will you potentially gain enough value to outweigh the potential harm? The potential benefits of attracting and hiring a top-flight candidate for a critical position will almost certainly overcome the concerns that you may have over a competitor having access to this information about a gap in your organization. Remember that your competitors may not even be using the Internet to study you – indeed, they may not be studying you at all!

Once the positions are posted on your site, you may find that you're getting resumes that reference seeing your posting somewhere else. It's not uncommon for sites that serve job seekers to visit your Web pages and "scrape" the content into their own listings. Some people regard this as an unethical practice, but you may find that it simply constitutes free advertising. Many of the scraper sites will remove your postings on request, if you decide that they're not doing you any favors.

2. Using national recruiting Web sites

When a job seeker first starts considering a new position, the first place he or she will often visit will be a major job posting Web site. Some of the top-rated sites are www.monster.com, www.vault.com, hotjobs.yahoo.com and www.careerjournal.com. If you'd like to ensure that you're in the hunt for the best candidates, along with the larger organizations, it may be worth the time and money to post your positions to one of these sites.

In addition, you can generally pay to gain access to the resumes that job seekers have posted to these sites. Here, you can find people who precisely meet your requirements, and then *you* can contact *them*. No more stacks of resumes to sort through in the aftermath of a newspaper ad!

3. Using local online recruiting opportunities

Check your local newspapers' Web sites to see what they offer in the area of online job listings. While these sites are typically much less sophisticated than the national sites, they're also much more geographically focused.

If you don't usually look outside of your local area, this option can provide an ideal balance between cost and reach. On the other hand, these listings are available to folks who are looking to relocate to your area even more easily than the paper edition.

Pay close attention to how your candidates will respond to listings online. If the newspaper offers a response form, take a close look at it yourself, to be sure that it reflects the professional appearance you want to maintain throughout your online presence.

4. Following up with candidates

When a candidate sends his or her resume to you via email (or via your Web site), again recall the cardinal rule of business email – acknowledge immediately, and answer soon.

Confirming with the candidate that the resume arrived intact is the polite thing to do, and it may spare you follow-up phone calls and emails. However, be cautious about replying to a business email address where the job seeker may still be employed. All too many larger companies scan their employees' email, which could lead to an awkward moment (such as sudden termination) for a surreptitious candidate.

Most job-hunters will be glad to hear from you via email. It can also be a great way to contact an elusive candidate – telephone calls aren't always caught, and messages can be too easily lost, but email almost always makes its way to the recipient.

If you do find a great candidate, and you write a formal offer letter, the original should still be physically given to your new employee, either in person or through the postal mail. Keep in mind that unless its encrypted, email is more akin to a postcard than to a sealed letter, and you probably wouldn't consider putting compensation details where the candidate's postman could see them at a glance.

Assessing Results

How many resumes do you now receive in electronic form? How quickly after a posting does the first resume appear? Are you getting higher quality candidates to consider? Are you able to hire more quickly? The answers to these questions will help you to fully gauge the success of this project in improving your business results.

What's Next?

Based on your experience with posting positions online, you may have gained some insights that will help you make better use of your competitors' online job postings. It may be worthwhile to go through Project 6, if you haven't already done so.

Project 11:
Analyzing Web Traffic

One of the most interesting ways in which the Web differs from other marketing avenues is in how well you can trace your prospects' route through your content. With good traffic analysis, you can see not only which efforts are working best to drive visitors into your Web site, but you can also see how well the Web site is serving their needs.

You can also find bottlenecks that may be causing them to give up and leave. Better that you find these by looking at a few Web logs than by wondering later why your site turned out to be such a flop! By examining how your visitors navigate your site, you can help to anticipate their needs – or help them find features that they've overlooked.

Prerequisites

In order to analyze Web traffic, you must have a Web site, of course. For some of the analysis tools, you will need access to the raw log files from your Web server. If your Web host cannot give you access to these files, you can look at some alternative tools.

Cost projections

Your software costs will probably range from zero, if a free solution is adequate to your analysis needs, to about $300 per year.

In addition to the software costs, you should plan on spending 10 to 40 hours in getting the analysis initially set up. Either way you go, you should plan to spend around 1 to 2 hours per week to review and act on the analysis, while you're actively watching your Web traffic.

Goals

Web traffic analysis will enable you to pinpoint opportunities to improve your Web site's technology, design and implementation. Seizing these opportunities will increase the likelihood that a visitor will become a lead, and that the lead will become a customer. As a reminder, a higher-quality lead reduces the cost of sale (and may increase average order size), both of which drive profitability.

Procedures

1. Select and set up analysis tools

As you embark on this project, you have a basic choice to make. You can either manage your own traffic analysis system, or you can use an ASP ("application service provider")-based system, which is managed by third parties on their own systems. (See Project 24 for more about this model of software deployment.)

Managing your own system gives you a great deal of flexibility, as well as total control over your analysis data. It works by examining the raw (and largely unintelligible) data in your Web server log files, pulling out the relevant patterns in the usage that is recorded in them. The system then generates fairly clear reports on the traffic it's analyzed.

An ASP-based system typically works by having you insert a small piece of code into each page that you want analysis on. This code reports traffic back to the ASP system, which then performs similar analysis and generates similar reports. Many ISPs include an ASP solution in your Web hosting package, though these may or may not adequately suit your needs.

If you cannot gain access to your Web log files, the choice is pretty easy – and an ASP system is the obvious solution. The same choice is self-evident if you have no desire to establish and maintain yet another software package at your site, or you have an inadequate solution provided with your hosting package. In addition, most ASP systems will allow monthly billing, at reasonable rates.

On the other hand, you will sacrifice some flexibility in formatting and selecting the reports, and some ASP solutions require the addition of special code to every tracked Web page, which adds administrative overhead. You may also prefer not to entrust your sensitive Web traffic data to a third party, although it's worth noting that they are closely bound by your contract with them to keep your information confidential.

You can find tools that will provide a good deal of basic capability for little or no cost; you can look on your favorite search engine for the search terms "web stats" or "log analysis" to find the current offerings in this space. Read the terms and conditions carefully, to be sure that you understand how these "free" services are being supported, so that you don't get any nasty surprises.

If you opt for a commercial package, be sure to read reviews and examine sample outputs. This is a rapidly evolving area of technology, and it's worth a little work up front to be sure that you're getting the solution that best suits your needs.

With either sort of system, you will have the ability to exclude any parts of your Web site for which you don't want analysis, but as a start, you should probably analyze everything.

2. Understand the results

Once your analysis tool is set up, you can start to view the reports that it generates. There are a couple of key pieces of information that nearly all of these tools will include in their reports.

In order to measure the success of Project 9, one of the most rewarding data points that your analysis reports will give you is the referring page, or where your visitors came from on the Web. This lets you see what search engines your visitors are most likely to use, and what search terms have been successful for them.

In addition, you will see what other links on the Web are bringing visitors to your site. You'll probably find some surprises here – again, one of the strengths of the Web is the ability to include links from anywhere to anywhere. You should almost always welcome such links – they're all driving traffic your way. One exception is the case where a site is simply using images or other content hosted on your site on their own site, without any credit or links back to you. This doesn't benefit you in any way, but it does use your bandwidth. Your Web site manager may be able to offer solutions to this problem if it affects you.

You should closely examine the most popular pages that the analysis identifies. Your most-used pages should probably be made very readily available, perhaps even with a link on the home page. Of course, if your most popular pages are the home page and a few detail pages linked directly from your home page, then your site design is probably working exactly as your visitors need it to.

You'll also want to have a look at the top entry pages. This will tell you whether visitors are starting on your home page, or whether perhaps they've bookmarked something further down the hierarchy. If you see a strong pattern to these direct entry points, you should probably consider bringing the material folks are jumping to closer to the front page, so that all of your visitors can discover it.

Next, you should look at your top exit pages. If your site design is working well, you should see your contact page, or your information-request form (see Project 20) near the top of the list – this indicates that people are digesting the content on your site and deciding to take the next step, getting in touch with you. If you see a pattern of folks exiting somewhere in the middle of a deep hierarchy, you probably need to consider flattening the design of your site somewhat. If they're entering and exiting on your home page, this is probably not a good thing – it may be a clarion call to consider a site design overhaul.

Many of the tools also allow you to analyze the most common paths through your site. This is also a good way to gauge whether your visitors are navigating through the menus as you had envisioned. In some cases, you may find that your users have discovered a shortcut you didn't realize was there. The rest of your visitors may well benefit from making that shortcut more prominent.

Your analysis reports will probably also include information about peak usage times and days of the week. This data is primarily of use when your traffic volume is reaching the limits of your hardware and software systems. As a small business, "you should have such worries!" Of course, if your site has been wildly successful, these are measurements that are well worth keeping a close eye on.

Also worth keeping a close watch over are the error reports that your site visitors have caused. Some of these will represent badly-behaved software packages connecting to your site, but 404 (page not found) and 500 (general server error) messages may indicate pages missing or broken on your site – things that should be fixed, post-haste.

3. Act on the information

Web site analysis is not something that you do once, and then forget about. It's a tool that will become an integral part of your site promotion and revision process.

For site promotion activities, you can start to assemble an idea of what the return on investment is. If visitors from a given source cost twice to attract as much as those from another, but yield three times as many leads and four times the eventual sales, you can immediately see where to get the best bang for your marketing buck.

For your site design tasks, the analysis tools will be at their most valuable when you use them as part of an ongoing design improvement cycle. Measure how easily visitors are finding a given page, and then make an improvement to your navigation. Now, go back and verify that the change actually yielded an improvement.

By following this routine with every substantive change you make on your site, your Web design efforts can adhere to the Hippocratic creed of "first, do no harm." Unlike medicine, though, you can easily undo a change that has not led to the improvements you'd hoped for.

Assessing Results

It's hard to say where the greater value comes from Web site traffic analysis – improving your site promotion effectiveness or increasing the usability of the Web site itself. Both of these effects, however, will have the potential to achieve the goals outlined above.

If the reports show it, are you surprised at the geographic range your visitors hail from? Do you see opportunities to serve those distant prospects, or should your site clearly delineate what your target market is?

Are your visitors paying a lot of attention to a product or service that you had thought was of marginal interest? Does it merit investigating whether there's a latent demand in your market? What other opportunities will Web site traffic analysis uncover?

What's Next?

With an effective traffic analysis system in place, you can now consider moving ahead with a banner advertisement campaign, in Project 16. By analyzing the referrer information, you can very quickly determine which banners are working best and which placements are the most effective.

You should probably also revisit Project 8, where you built your Web site, with an eye toward making improvements, as mentioned in this project. Remember that a site makeover is something that should be approached with great caution – but it's better to find that out through traffic analysis than through profit-and-loss analysis. By the time the impact of a poor Web site shows up on your balance sheets, the damage is already done.

Project 12:
Getting a Faster Internet Connection

Dialup Internet access is usually sufficient for home use and is often enough when you're just getting started in business use. If you have multiple users at your place of business or if you just need to be able to use the Internet more quickly yourself, you will find yourself being tempted by the promises of greater Internet speed in various advertisements that you see.

In this project, you'll cut through the hype and decide whether a faster connection is worthwhile for your business and if so, what the benefits and drawbacks are to each of the major options available on the market today.

Prerequisites

You should have a personal computer, preferably with at least dialup Internet access. (You could skip Project 1 and jump right to this project for your first connection, but it may not be the most efficient use of your money when you're just getting started on the Internet.)

Cost projections

Depending on the option you select, your setup costs will range anywhere from nearly nothing to several thousand dollars, and monthly expenses will run between $50 and $2,500 (though the high end of this range is pretty unlikely to apply to a small business). If your business need justifies one of the very high-end solutions, you may also need to add staff to configure and maintain the additional hardware. If you will be networking multiple computers in order to take advantage of shared access to the Internet, be sure to budget for the expenses that will entail as well.

Some of the low-end solutions, on the other hand, may actually reduce your expenses, if you had established an additional phone line for data use. Your telecommunications provider may also offer attractive bundled prices, which can further reduce your expenses. In addition the increased efficiency of your organization's online activities should also be considered.

Goals

Most importantly, if your business has started to make substantial use of the Internet as a resource, increased speed will improve the efficiency of those efforts. This can provide a persuasive justification for a faster connection once you're heavily reliant on the Internet for your organization's daily activities.

You will probably be able to more nimbly make adjustments to your Web site, which could have a positive impact on the business metrics that you've already seen affected by that activity.

Procedures

1. Understand the options

There are a large number of options available for high-speed Internet connections. The most common include (in roughly increasing order of expense) cable modem, DSL, satellite and leased-line (T-1 and similar). All of the solutions mentioned below will free you from the irritation of waiting for a dialup connection to be established, as they are all "always on."

Your local cable TV franchise may be offering high-speed Internet connections over the same lines as your HBO and CNN are delivered. Many cable modem operators explicitly forbid the use of their services for business purposes. However if your local cable provider does permit you to use their services for your business, this can be a very attractive option.

In many cases, the monthly costs are comparable to that of a phone line plus a dialup ISP ($40 to $60), and the speeds are typically far better than dialup. In some cases, the special equipment needed is included in the bill, and the setup fees ($100 to $300) may even be waived, especially if you're willing to sign a year-long or longer contract. Service levels are comparable to what you see from other parts of your cable-TV franchise – that is to say, anywhere from mediocre to abominable.

DSL (sometimes referred to as ADSL, xDSL, or other variants) is the most common competitor to cable modem. The good news is that you don't have to deal with your cable franchise. The bad news is that you may have to contend with your phone company *and* a DSL-capable ISP (unless one firm provides both services).

Speed is in the same range as cable modem. There are, however, considerations that will affect the performance you see, primarily having to do with the physical distance of your installation from the phone company's nearest substation.

The expense of DSL is usually slightly higher than cable modem – be aware that some DSL offers may only list the cost of the connection and omit the charges for the ISP. You may also have the option to pay a higher fee for a faster connection. Overall, your costs for DSL will probably be between $50 and $750 per month depending on your region, the speed and the ISP options that you choose. Setup fees are similar to cable modem ($100 to $300), and may also be waived.

Both DSL and cable modem are usually only available in densely populated areas. If you're in an outlying region, you may want to investigate a satellite connection. Costs are again comparable to DSL ($100 to $300 per month), as is speed. You typically have to purchase the dish and other equipment, which makes your setup costs higher than with DSL or cable, rising into the $800 to $1,000 range.

Because your Internet traffic must travel to the satellite and back to Earth, every request you make on the Internet will have a slight delay, which will range from half a second to a full second. (The data is traveling around 50,000 miles, at the speed of light – quite a lot further than the few thousand miles that a land-based connection must navigate.)

If you're in a rural area, though, satellite Internet connectivity can be very attractive indeed. In the next few years, expect this to be one of the fastest-growing means of getting high-speed access, particularly with the coming addition of new satellite constellations which will drive competition – and competition is always good news for you as a consumer of a service.

Another option you can consider is leased-line solutions. These are typically the solutions used by mid-sized organizations, right up to the largest companies in the world. However, if your Internet efforts are a big enough part of your business, it might be worth the expense to step up to a solution in this class. You should also be aware of these solutions so that if a sales rep starts to push them on you, and they're not appropriate to your needs, you can be aware of that, as well.

A full T-1 line will have setup fees in the range of $300 to $600, and monthly expenses (depending on the bandwidth – the amount of data capacity – you need) will probably be between $750 and $2,500 per month. If you are seriously considering hosting your Web site on a computer at your location, you may be wise to consider a T-1 line as part of the expense of that move.

The advantages of a leased line are that you will have a very fast, dedicated connection, usually with high speeds available in both directions (critical if you're sending data from a Web server, as well as requesting it from other systems). A single T-1 line can usually serve the needs of several dozen employees simultaneously. You may also be able to use part of it to handle your voice telephone traffic. Cost is the main downside to this solution.

Even faster connections are also available as leased-line solutions; however, they are used almost exclusively by ISPs to carry their customers' traffic. If you need such a fast connection, you probably no longer need this book!

There are a few other possibilities hitting the market as of this writing – community wireless, power-line Internet, etc. A terrific source of information about these emerging solutions is www.broadbandreports.com, although this site is more focused on home use than on business use.

Another option that you may have seen advertised is "accelerators" for your dial-up account, promising up to a 5x boost to your dialup speed. This solution relies on the use of compression and removing content suspected of being advertisement. It has the significant disadvantage of still requiring you to establish your connection anew for each session of Internet usage, negating all of the benefits of always-on connectivity. Your browsing experience may also be compromised by the loss of graphics and other content incorrectly identified as being superfluous.

2. Get connected

Now that you understand your options, you should request quotes from the service providers you're interested in. Their sales staffs are motivated to answer your questions, so use them as a resource. Be aware, of course, that these people are also motivated to get your business, so you'll want to use the same caution that you would for any major business decision. Confirm that any quotes include all setup fees and equipment costs, as well as any required additional services. Be sure that you understand the length of commitment you're making, and the penalties for early cancellation.

Once you sign up, the provider you've selected will almost always send technicians out to your location to set up the necessary equipment and connect your computer to it. Be sure that you have prepared easy access to the computer. In some cases, you may even have to relocate it, so that you can more readily connect to the feed from your ISP. Their sales and technical staff can probably help guide you in this regard.

3. Security

Now that you are connected full-time, often with a permanent IP address (the number that other computers use to communicate with yours), you must consider the security of your system. If you do not secure your system, it can and likely will be hijacked by unscrupulous denizens of the Internet's darker corners. Most of the spam and hacker attacks you see and hear about are launched from hijacked machines.

Although it's nearly impossible to completely secure a system from a skilled hacker absolutely determined to compromise it, you can make it difficult enough to deter the casual or unskilled hacker. Think of it as you would locking your car in a big-city downtown. Nothing can make it completely secure – but you can encourage the miscreants to move on to an easier target.

You will probably want to invest in some form of firewall. Roughly speaking, the quality of protection afforded by a firewall will rise with its expense. However, there are other factors, as well. An expensive, but widely used firewall system may have known weaknesses which can be readily exploited by a knowledgeable hacker.

You can get software that will reside on a single computer, securing it from malicious visitors. If you have multiple computers sharing the connection (see below), you should consider a dedicated firewall system. For small networks or single computers, there are devices that operate as a firewall at relatively low expense (under $100), and which may also offer other capabilities, such as connection sharing or even networking.

Microsoft also includes a firewall and connection sharing capability in their latest releases of Windows. It has the advantage of being built into the operating system, but, since it's so widely distributed, it's also likely to be a major target for the digital vandals of the world.

As part of connecting a larger network to the Internet, you should probably discuss a more sophisticated firewall solution with your network administrator or ISP. These systems will usually consist of a dedicated computer with specialized software running on it. They have the advantage of being much more flexible than their smaller brethren, but at a higher cost, both in cash and in the expertise necessary to establish and maintain them.

The most important action you can take to improve the security of any Internet connection, though, is to keep all of your systems as current as possible. As security flaws are discovered in the various software and computer systems that you use, their manufacturers will invariably make updates available to address the flaws.

Microsoft Windows and most other modern operating systems offer a means of automatically checking for security updates. Be sure that you faithfully utilize this capability, both on your server systems and on your desktop and laptop machines.

4. Sharing the connection

If you have multiple computers at your location, having a high-speed, always-on connection makes it practical for all of your PCs to have access to the Internet. There are a number of solutions to help you make this happen. For an easy, all-in-one solution, you can find dedicated devices that will allow you to share one Internet connection with a workgroup of up to a couple dozen computers.

If you have more PCs than this, you may already have an internal network established. Discuss with the person responsible for this network what you might need to do to give your network users access to the public Internet. Anticipate the need for a firewall (as discussed above), as well as some configuration of each computer that will have access.

If you do not already have a network, the expenses and process to establish one are beyond the scope of this book, but there are plenty of good resources available to you for more information. Check your bookstore (online or local), and do research through your favorite search engine for the details of what to expect.

One note of caution regarding wireless networks: While they're wonderfully easy to set up, and they make sharing your connection simple and natural, you must secure them to avoid sharing your connection with anyone who happens to be within range. Not only will such "visitors" use your bandwidth, but they may be able to gain access to the machines on your network. You can think of it as carefully locking all of the doors and windows in your house, but leaving the back porch standing wide open.

Fortunately, it's easy to secure a wireless network; check the documentation of the device you're using to enable wireless connectivity for instructions on setting up WEP ("wired equivalent privacy") protection for your network. Be aware that this technology, like any security technology, is not an absolute safeguard for your network, but it does provide a measure of protection.

5. Employee usage

Once you have a high-speed connection to the Internet, and you've made this available to your employees, you will probably need to confront the issues of how they use this tool. Bear in mind that you're making this available to further your business goals, and so you can regard it just as you would any other facility you make available to your staff.

High-speed Internet access in particular can tempt users to use resources that may not be appropriate for a business environment. It's a known fact that some of the most profitable businesses on the Internet serve the desires of consumers of pornography and gambling services – and that their usage is heaviest during business hours. It's unlikely that this use of the Internet is in the best interests of your organization's success.

You may be able to partially address this issue through using your firewall system to block some objectionable material, but it's nearly impossible to block all of it. Most firewall systems will also allow you to monitor how your employees are using the Internet. Consult the documentation or speak with the person who manages your network for information on your options in this regard.

You should also consider the ramifications of file-sharing systems such as BitTorrent and Kazaa, which are frequently used to share materials in violation of copyright law. Worse, it's all too common for spyware and viruses to be spread through these systems. Part of granting employees access to the Internet should be installation of software to protect against spyware and other "malware."

In any case, most businesses have an Internet usage policy that clearly lays out that Internet access is provided in order to allow employees to more effectively do their jobs, that it is a company resource, and that there are acceptable and unacceptable uses of that resource. You can inform your employees that their usage is subject to monitoring, and that abuse will have serious consequences.

Think of it as you would your telephone system. If an employee started using 900 lines on your dime, you would probably want to stop them from doing this. If an employee calls home during a break, it probably doesn't have a negative impact on your business. A reasonable Internet usage policy will support your company's goals without making your employees feel as if you distrust them.

Be aware, too, that there may be consequences for your organization of turning a blind eye to particularly inappropriate usage. The expense and other effects of litigation under a wide variety of Federal, state and local statutes regarding harassment can represent a crushing blow to your business plan.

Of course, this is a field where there are ongoing and lively discussions. Viewpoints range from radicals on one end of the spectrum who think that any monitoring or limitations on employee Internet usage is draconian, to radicals on the other end who think that no employee should be trusted with access. You will need to examine your own business philosophy and knowledge of your employees and make a reasonable decision of your own.

6. Internet telephony

Another usage to consider for your new bandwidth is "voice over internet protocol," or VoIP -- essentially, using your Internet connection to connect to a digital telephone network. You may even be able to retain your current telephone number, greatly reduce your long distance costs, and eliminate your ordinary phone line, all in one move. (This may help in the financial decision to go to a broadband connection.)

Your costs will probably be in the range of $35 to $100 per month, per line of service, depending upon the features that you want. Some of the providers give you the ability to have local phone numbers in a number of places at once, so that if you have customers, say, across the state line, you can give them a local number to call, instead of a long-distance or toll-free number.

VoIP does, however, have some drawbacks. For one thing, it needs a lot of bandwidth to deliver good sound quality. With insufficient bandwidth, your calls can sound like you have a bad cell connection. Too, it is subject to the vagaries of your Internet connection. In case of a power outage or Internet failure, you could find yourself on a cell phone trying to get in touch with your utility providers.

You will usually get a relatively small device to attach to your network, into which you can then plug your standard telephone. You might even be able to plug in a standard telephone network, giving several extensions service -- check with your provider, though. If you have an existing PBX system, you will probably need a more advanced solution, and your costs will rise correspondingly.

Assessing Results

Have a look at your overall productivity as the primary metric that will be moved by the transition to a faster connection. The ability to make swift changes to your Web site can also have a business impact, although this may be more difficult to quantify.

If you've been able to consolidate some of your telecommunications expenses through this project, the savings you see there will go straight to the bottom line.

What's Next?

With a dedicated Internet connection, it becomes very practical to establish Internet email addresses for each of your employees. As email is often cited as the most important advance made possible by the Internet, adding this capability to your business is covered in Project 13.

Project 13:
Employee Email Accounts

In a business where a number of employees have their own Internet-connected computers, it makes sense to set each of them up with their own email addresses. This enables them to converse directly with customers and partners, rather than having everything go through one shared account.

When you consider that "markets are conversations," as has been observed, it makes a lot of sense to enable those conversations to take place as naturally as possible. By facilitating direct communication between your people and your customers and suppliers, you effectively extend the walls of your enterprise to encompass these people outside of your defined organization. Powerful stuff!

Prerequisites

You'll want a dedicated, high-speed Internet connection and access to a personal computer for each person who will have email. It's possible to set up strictly Web-based email for your employees, which eliminates the need for a dedicated connection, but this undermines much of the value of email as a communications medium.

If you don't have a domain name, this would be a good time to go to Project 8 and learn how to establish one; otherwise your employees' business email addresses may be indistinguishable from home email addresses.

Cost projections

If you have only a few employees online, you may be able to use an application service provider (ASP) to manage hosted "POP3" compliant email for you. ("POP3" just means "post office protocol 3" – the standard for Internet email) Your Web hosting provider may supply this service at a reasonable cost (they may even include it as part of your service package), or there are third-party providers who can also fill this need. If you are able to take advantage of this option, budget some time (4 to 12 hours) to set up all of your users to access their email, and budget between $150 and $500 per year for the hosting fees, if it's not included in your existing service.

Another common option is to establish your own email server in house. You should budget between $750 and $5,000 for an email server computer, up to $2,000 for email server software, and about a week's time to deploy and troubleshoot the system. You may profit by simply hiring an expert to handle your deployment; figure on $1,000 to $3,000 for that.

Goals

Sales staff efficiency will likely rise dramatically, particularly for sales outside of your immediate area. Email is a great leveler for working across time zones. Post-sales support costs will probably drop, as your support staff can make use of templates. (See Project 21 for more information on this powerful email management technique.)

All of the benefits ascribed to effectively managing your customer email apply in spades to this project. In addition, the internal use of email will eliminate the need for paper memos and increase the efficiency of internal communications. If you've opted to host your own email server, most servers include powerful scheduling systems and collaboration tools, all of which will make your entire staff more efficient when they're used correctly. Bear in mind that you may need to plan for additional training to get the most out of such capabilities.

1. Do you need an email server?

For a business that needs to give email access to only few employees, and does not need group scheduling capabilities, you may be able to sidestep building a dedicated in-house server. Discuss with your Web hosting provider or ISP what options are available and what the costs will be. If you already have a hosted Web site, a certain number POP3-compliant email accounts may already be included in your hosting fee, with more probably available for a small incremental cost. If you determine that this option will work for you, skip ahead to Step 3.

If you have more than about 25 employees who will need to have access to email, you should probably consider going ahead and building a dedicated email server. Over the long term, the additional management capabilities and security of having your own system manage your email will probably be worthwhile.

2. Select and install email server system

This is one of those tasks where the use of a consultant may save you a great deal of difficulty. There are several industry-standard email server packages that compete heavily for the small-business market.

Some have the benefit of superb setup and maintenance tools, but this capability usually comes at a price. On the other hand, systems which come with little or no initial cash outlay may well cost you a great deal of time and effort to set up and maintain, erasing your savings in an instant.

In the end, your decision should be guided by which systems would best integrate with the rest of the software that you're using to manage your business. If you've been a pure Microsoft shop up to now, then Microsoft's Exchange Server is a pretty easy decision to make. Likewise, if you're running your business on a Lotus suite or on a Linux-based desktop system, there are packages which are designed from the ground up to operate in those environments.

Whatever you choose, consider carefully the decision to add backup capability to this business-critical system. More than one small business has suffered weeks of lost productivity when an email server failed, leaving employees out of touch and losing critical messages from lost email archives.

After you take delivery of all of the hardware and software for your new email server, follow the manufacturer's instructions to complete the setup and initial configuration. You will probably need assistance from the person who handles your network in setting up the Internet connection for this machine, and from your ISP in setting up the mapping from its numeric address to the domain address. (This will let you be known as "jsmith@somecompany.com," instead of "jsmith@192.213.13.24." Minor detail, right?)

3. Set up users

When it's time to set up the individual user accounts on your chosen email system, you should consider what sort of naming convention to follow. Bear in mind that only letters, numbers, dashes and periods are permitted in Internet email addresses. There are some rationales and trends behind some of the more common conventions, but it tends to be a matter of personal preference.

Many businesses simply use a "first initial-last name" convention. Thus, John Smith becomes jsmith@somecompany.com. Others, following a fairly new trend (particularly at larger companies), use the first name-last name ("johnsmith@somecompany.com"), or first name-dot-last name ("john.smith@somecompany.com"). Very large companies may even include the middle initial, for clarity.

A few smaller companies just use the employee's first name or last name, and a very few companies use first name-last initial ("johns@somecompany.com"). Whatever scheme you settle on, be aware that some names will give unfortunate email addresses if you are too slavish about following the standards. In addition, some email systems may constrain how long you can make the account name, which may prevent you from being able to fully implement some of the options.

It's also worth considering how much typing you want to ask of your employees' correspondents. (Remember that a typo can be less of an irritant, and more of a disaster when information is misaddressed as a result.) And, of course, most systems will allow you to assign multiple addresses to one employee, so you can have the more informal "john@somecompany.com" as well as the standardized address, if you like.

The main reason for settling on some convention or another is to enable your customers to easily reach the employees they want to talk to. If they have to remember that John is "jsmith@somecompany.com," but Sandy is "sandraj2@somecompany.com," the opportunities for error increase tremendously.

After you have set up the accounts, you just need to set up the client software on each machine. Follow the software provider's documentation and on-line help on this. If you've used an outside mail service (and in some cases, with an internal email server), you will need to use POP3. In any event, the one thing to be sure of is that you set up the client software so that it checks for new messages frequently and alerts the user when an email arrives.

4. Email best practices

Review Project 2 with each of your email-enabled employees, stressing the importance of the "acknowledge immediately, answer soon" doctrine. Remember that many businesses fail to respond in a timely manner – or at all – to their email. This is an easy place to set yourself apart from the competition!

Be sure that all email users are aware of netiquette. A particularly common violation of good email etiquette in internal email systems is carbon-copying ("cc'ing") a whole raft of people, when only one or two need the information in a message. This breach is then multiplied when someone on the list hits "reply to all," instead of just selecting the people who need to see the reply.

Review the practices of "safe computing" with your employees, as well. Attachments from unexpected sources should *never* be opened, and even those from trusted sources should be subjected to a virus screener. They should understand how important it is to leave such systems running, as well -- like the annoying smoke detector with the batteries ripped out, an antivirus program turned off is no protection at all.

5. Abuse prevention

Just like widespread Internet access, personal employee email is subject to abuse. See Project 12 for ideas about setting reasonable, common sense policies around Internet use generally, and apply similar standards to employee email. Again, be particularly sensitive to the potential for offensive material to be circulated on your systems; some companies have been found liable in harassment cases for failing to adequately discourage such misuse.

Remind all email users that anything they send can be forwarded – sometimes beyond where they had foreseen. Plenty of promising opportunities have been lost as a scathing or slanderous email was forwarded to its subject. This is an easily avoided "career limiting move!"

Assessing Results

To measure the success of this project, have a look at the volume of conversations that take place between your employees and your customers and business partners. As a small bonus, you may see your long-distance telephone bill decline somewhat. Overnight mail expenses may also drop, depending on the nature of your business. (Some businesses require that physical documents still be quickly transported between locations.)

Longer term, examine your sales volume and cost of sales. As volume rises and cost of sales drops, the profitability of each sales transaction improves dramatically. Have a look, too, at customer retention and repeat business. Like so many other of the projects in this book, both of these metrics will probably be positively impacted by the advent of employee email.

Finally, look at the trends in your internal communications. Are meetings being avoided, as information is communicated via email instead? Are communications between all levels of the organization moving more smoothly? Are overall efficiency and employee productivity rising?

What's Next?

With an employee email system in place, you can now look at implementing an email newsletter, in Project 15. In addition, email is closely related to Project 19, in which you'll establish a customer forum.

Project 14:
Gathering Customer Feedback

Part of the power of the Web is that it's always on – you can receive critical information from your customers even when everyone in your company is happily snoring. Setting up these important capabilities will add interactivity to your Web site, turning it into much more than just a static marketing piece.

Prerequisites

You must have a Web site, and it must be capable of handling email forms. Check with your Web designer if you're not sure that you have this capability. You must also have at least one email in-box, and an always-on Internet connection will greatly enhance the value of this capability.

Cost projections

Initial setup of this tool on your site will probably take 10 to 20 hours of effort (figure $500 to $1,500 if you contract for it); management of the information gathered will become part of your email routine (see Project 2).

Goals

This project should positively impact customer communications, which may allow you to more quickly innovate. This can lead to greater market share and penetration. Like the other projects that focused on communication with your customers, it will probably drive customer loyalty and repeat business, as well as referrals.

Project 14: Gathering Customer Feedback

Procedures

1. Understanding Web forms

Any time you've submitted an order on Amazon, checked your email on Hotmail, or sent nearly any information into a Web site, you've used a form. The specific type of form this project will discuss is one of the simpler ones – it merely takes the entries it collects and turns them into an email. The strength of a Web-based email form, though, is that you can request specific pieces of information – even require them, if you feel that your business process justifies it – and receive that information in a structured way.

In order to understand how this works, you'll need to review a little bit about how the Web works. When you visit a Web site, there are at least two pieces of software communicating with each other. Your browser operates within your own machine, and it speaks to a Web server across the Internet.

Your browser knows how to ask for specific pages and then display them, using the Web's *lingua franca*, HTML. Modern browsers also know how to handle other sorts of content, such as images, video and audio clips and so forth.

Web servers know how to receive requests, and, in most cases, serving those requests is a simple matter of retrieving a file from a hard drive, formatting it for transmission over the Internet and sending it off. However, some requests cause the server to run software of varying complexity, to perform tasks of varying sophistication.

Turning a Web form into an email involves all of these capabilities, all working together. The visitor requests the page with the form on it. The server retrieves that file, formats and sends it, and the browser then receives and displays it. After the visitor has filled it in, the browser may have instructions to check it over for completion prior to sending, or that check may be deferred to the server.

When the form is submitted to the server, this causes the server to run a small piece of software that takes the input, formats it into an email, and then sends it according to the instructions in the software. Prior to doing this, it may check the form for completeness and return it to the browser with a message to the visitor, informing them of what information is still needed.

This may all sound very complicated, but as mentioned above, it's one of the more common tasks handled by Web forms, so there is a lot of "prior art" to draw upon.

2. Building the feedback page(s)

The first task is to decide how you want to use the form. For the purposes of this project, we'll consider a very basic feedback form. You can extend this same concept to accept support inquiries, accept product suggestions, or manage customer forum subscriptions (see Project 19).

The first thing to do is to determine what you will need to do in order to support a form emailer. If your site is hosted on someone else's system, they probably have a specific capability to manage forms and email. (It may be referred to in their documentation or online help as "formmail" or a "form mailer.")

If, after examining the documentation for your Web site host, and even discussing it with your site designer, you determine that there's no capability, you may need to consider changing hosts. Alternatively, you can look for a service that will handle just the form mailing, and allow you to leave the rest of your site where it is.

If you're hosting on your own system, of course, you should have no trouble with this capability. The exact technology you use will depend on your specific Web server software, but the software provider's documentation will almost certainly include a clear example of how to support a form mailer. Failing this, there is add-on software available for just about any Web server to fill this need, and the externally-hosted service is an option here, as well.

Next, you or your Web designer will need to actually create the form in HTML, adhering to the look-and-feel of the rest of your site. In addition to the information that your user needs to enter, the form handler may require the inclusion of other data, perhaps in hidden fields on the page.

It's always a good idea to visually indicate to your user what fields will be required – it saves a lot of aggravation. An asterisk, or a contrasting color on the text describing what to enter in the required field, are the commonly used methods of accomplishing this.

If you want to get very fancy, you can add some script to the page to check the form for completion. This is the code that the browser will be asked to run, before it ever sends the data back to the server for handling. Alternatively, your form mailer may have an easy way to accomplish the same thing. In either case, be very sure that the visual indicators you've given match what the code is going to do.

In either the hidden fields, or in the form handling code on the server, you will need to specify an email address to send the collected data on to. As a general rule, it's a poor practice to specify an individual's email address for this purpose. Personnel changes are usually disruptive enough, without having to go and change hard-coded software as well. It's most common to establish a generic email address that someone is then responsible for monitoring closely, or which is then forwarded to a specific person by the email server.

Follow the directions with the form mailer software you're using to install the form page and its handler on your Web server. It's also a good idea to have an acknowledgement page that tells your visitor that you appreciate their input, and that lays out what your standards are for response times.

Once you have it all set up, before you link it into the rest of your Web site, test, test, test. Try every conceivable combination of incomplete, invalid and otherwise faulty input, and ensure that the page handles it all, without giving a confusing or misleading error report. Using the information you've gathered by analyzing your log files in Project 11, test with the most common browser and operating system combinations your visitors use. Check to ensure that what you enter is received at the other end, accurately and completely.

Try to simulate problems with the Internet connection, your email system, and so forth, with an eye towards ensuring that no valid feedback, once submitted, will ever be lost. At the very least, that the user should be told that there is a problem, and their feedback may not have reached you. Nothing's worse than having to deal with a user whose important inquiry was misplaced in cyber-space.

3. Procedures for feedback

When you receive feedback from your Web form, you should normally treat it with the same importance as you would any other direct customer email. The "acknowledge immediately, answer soon" standard applies especially well to this sort of communication. As a further enhancement to your form mailer, you may even want to build in acknowledgement, so that the sender has an additional level of confidence that you have received the feedback and will act on it. (Including a copy of the original feedback is also a good means for helping folks track down spurious submissions or other abuse.)

Unless you've chosen to accept anonymous feedback, you should always respond as soon as possible. The person responsible for monitoring the feedback mailbox should be encouraged to forward messages from customers to whomever in the company can resolve the issues they contain. If the issue cannot be resolved, someone in authority should explain in a non-confrontational way why this is the case.

All of the rules of netiquette (see Project 2) apply to feedback sent from your Web site – even if your customers fail to observe them. Remember that "kill 'em with kindness" is a good practice in dealing with an irate customer – particularly online, where your responses can be instantly shared with the world.

The reason for these warnings and reminders will probably soon become evident to you, once you have this capability available. For some reason, many people feel that a Web form, addressed as it is to an unnamed, faceless person, is an open invitation to be far harsher than they would ever be in addressing a known individual. The faster you can remind them that you're only interested in resolving their issue, and that they are actually dealing with a real, live human, the faster they'll return to their normal approach. (Of course, what "normal" means will depend upon the nature of your customer base.)

4. Extending the concept

Once you've mastered the basics of turning Web form input into email, you can create a form for prospects to use to request more information. Doubtless you've received emails that didn't include enough information to act on – no name, no phone number, and so on.

With a Web form, you can be certain to gather the data you need to properly follow up with a prospect. A few words of caution are warranted, however. If you are gathering personal information of any sort, you should be sure to include a privacy statement. It's a very good idea to apply for and display a TRUSTe privacy seal. For more information on this well-recognized program, visit their site at www.truste.org.

If your prospects might include children under the age of 13, the Children's Online Privacy Protection Act (COPPA) places stringent limitations on what information you can gather, and how you can use that information. The TRUSTe site also contains information on this law, and resources to help you comply with it.

There are also regulations to be aware of if you might be dealing with customers in the European Union; again, the TRUSTe site, or a bit of research at your favorite search engine will give you the information that you need in order to avoid running afoul of the requirements for that market.

Assessing Results

Your customers most likely know their needs even better than you do. They may even see ways for you to serve their needs that you're not yet aware of. By making it as easy as possible for them to communicate with you, you can learn from their insights and seize market opportunities that they've identified.

In addition, if you get a reputation for being responsive to feedback, this will be yet another reason for your customers to give you more of their business and to refer their colleagues to you, as well. It may be challenging to discern exactly what the impact of a Web-based feedback form is on your business, but over the long term, it will reap dividends beyond what you can foresee.

What's Next?

Now that you've taken your first foray into Web-based forms, you can probably see a lot of potential applications for them. Project 20 will show you how use a more sophisticated form to collect lead information directly from your customers, increasing the chances that you will have valid and complete information to act on.

Project 15:
Setting Up an Email Newsletter

While spam is an unwelcome intruder in email inboxes every-where, an informative, useful newsletter will nearly always get a friendly reception. Periodic newsletters also drive Web traffic and business, acting as a gentle reminder that your company stands ready to solve your customers' problems. They're also another opportunity to ask for feedback from your customers – always a good idea!

Prerequisites

A high-speed Internet connection and a Web site will both make this project much more successful. You must have an email inbox to handle replies and inquiries that the newsletter raises. A Web site to which you can direct readers for more information or to act on offers in your newsletters is a very good idea.

Cost projections

To ensure the success of this project, you should endeavor to collect email addresses from as many of your customers and prospects as possible. If you've already been getting this informa-tion, you are well positioned to begin. If not, then you may want to budget for a clerical temporary worker to call your customer base and collect email addresses.

Establishing a format will probably require 4 to 8 hours of your time. Content gathering and formatting time will vary, according to your needs, but you should probably allow for a couple of hours per issue. Depending upon whether you want to drive traffic to your Web site, you might want to budget some time to make tie-in pages for each issue of the newsletter, so that you can accurately gauge your success in increasing site traffic.

You may also need to budget some money to provide mailing-list services, if you decide to use one of these offerings; typical costs are based on the size of your subscriber list and the frequency of your mailings. Figure between $5 and $25 per month; be aware that some providers may charge setup fees, on top of this.

Goals

Because an email newsletter is a prime means of implementing "trickle marketing," this project will probably have its biggest impact on repeat business, as well as in terms of reviving dead opportunities.

Trickle marketing is the practice of more-or-less constantly reminding your customers and prospects of your potential value to them, rather than engaging in grandiose large marketing pushes. It's a proven and powerful method in many large businesses, and, via the Internet, a small business can also use it.

Procedures

1. Getting permission

Please review the comments about "spam" in Project 2. It's absolutely essential that you get your customers' and prospects' explicit permission to send them email, particularly when the purpose of the email is very specifically for marketing.

Under no circumstances should you send your email newsletters to people whose email addresses you've gleaned from Web sites, newsgroups (see Project 18), or other third-party resources. This is clearly spam and, as mentioned in Project 2, it can cost you fines and your Internet connection, not to mention besmirching your online reputation.

When you have an established business relationship with someone (either as a customer, a prospect, or a partner), sending unsolicited commercial email to him or her is something of a gray area. Better to avoid doubt, and only send to those people who

114

have clearly said, "Yes, I'd like to periodic email messages from your organization."

Your market may be one where not many of your customers have email addresses, although the penetration of email in the US marketplace is approaching a saturation point where it's nearly universal. If, however, you cannot get addresses (or permission) for a substantial portion of your customer base, you might be better served to consider a paper newsletter instead.

You should get into the habit, whenever you get an email address from a contact, of asking whether it's okay to send them an occasional email about your firm. If you ask this question on a Web form, the default answer should be "no" – too many people skip past questions on forms, and are then surprised when you add them to your subscription list. If a Web visitor goes to the trouble to select a "yes" answer to this question, then there should be no question as to whether or not they intended to hear from you.

You may also want to add a newsletter subscription option to the home page of your site. It's becoming very common to see a small input box and a "subscribe!" button on the sites of smart businesses, and this is a terrific way to both gather good email addresses, and demonstrate that you're offering a newsletter as a service to your marketplace.

If you want the extra verifiability of what's known as a "double opt-in," you can send a quick email to all new subscribers (or have your systems do so), asking them to confirm that they do want to be added to your newsletter mailing list. When you mail to a list with a double opt-in of this nature, it's very difficult to accuse you of sending unwanted messages.

If you don't currently have good email address coverage in your customer database, it's well worth your while to have someone collect it. At every contact point, your customers should be asked to give you their email address, and permission to use it. You may also decide to go ahead and actively contact them, via phone or postcard, and ask. Though it may incur a short-term expense, the returns over the long term will be great.

2. Creating a format

When a customer receives your newsletter, several things should be immediately apparent to them: who it's from, why they're receiving it, and how to tell you to stop sending it. You will be well served to further establish a standard set of content that you'll include. Standard "columns" in the newsletter are a great way to tie one issue together with the next. Another item that you should usually include is a request for feedback. Your subscribers will tell you what they liked and didn't like – you have only to ask them.

Encourage readers to forward the newsletter to their colleagues, and include information on how to subscribe, for those readers looking at a forwarded copy of the message. By providing a useful resource to your market, your email newsletter will help to introduce your organization to a wider audience than ever.

One decision that you will have to make is whether to send just a plain-text newsletter, or to try a full HTML version. HTML gives you a lot more capability in terms of formatting, and can even offer you the ability to very accurately determine how successful the mailing was, but it's a newer technology. It's usually a good call to go with a lowest common denominator, in order to maximize your potential audience.

Furthermore, creating an HTML newsletter requires that you know a fair amount about HTML, and really leveraging its power will require some pretty advanced knowledge of the format. If you have someone available who's developed this skill, it might be worth considering – but even then, proceed with caution and respect for your less technology-savvy subscribers.

3. Generating content

Your newsletter should be brief enough to skim within a few seconds, and to read from start to finish in less than three minutes. Think about the way that you use email yourself. When you receive a message, you probably scan it very quickly to decide if it merits reading, and you usually can't spend more than a minute or two on it, at the most. Your subscribers will be no different.

Typically, no more than 3 to 5 articles should be in any newsletter, including regular features, and probably even including the administrative information about unsubscribing and so forth. It's a great idea to include a very brief "table of contents" at the top of the newsletter. All of this demonstrates to your subscribers that you respect their time – and they are more likely to welcome your messages, rather than ignoring them, or unsubscribing.

The items you include in your newsletter should be timely – in fact, many organizations avoid having a set schedule for their newsletters, and instead issue one when there's enough material to justify it. New products or services, changes to existing ones, news that affects your marketplace and general news about significant events for your business are all great topics to cover.

You could also cover the most frequent questions your sales and support staff are fielding. Some of your audience may have the same questions, but just not have gotten around to asking. By covering material like this in a newsletter, you can avoid those calls entirely, saving everyone money and time.

Like your Web site, you must be absolutely certain that you have permission to use any material that you haven't created entirely yourself. This permission may be somewhat easier to secure than it might be for your Web site, because of the more limited distribution and lifespan of a newsletter. However, it may well be simpler all around to create the content yourself.

As you create the articles, remember that the overarching goal of the newsletter is to remind your subscribers that you offer solutions to their problems. If you're in a service business, case studies are tremendous for newsletters, as they illustrate how your organization has solved a real problem for a real customer. Work closely with customers you feature in case studies, getting their approval and feedback. Some customers may prefer anonymity, but if you can name them, it makes the case study all the more powerful.

A very useful approach to drive people onto your Web site, where you then have the opportunity to deepen your business relationships with them, is to only include a headline and some teaser text in the emailed newsletter, and post the full article online. If you opt for this approach, you will need to be absolutely certain that the online articles are posted and available before you send the newsletter. (Overlooking this timing is a common-enough mistake.)

Even if you decide not to use this method, be on the lookout for opportunities to include a link to your site in various articles in the newsletter. If you're discussing a recent change to a product or service, a link for the reader to follow for full background information is a perfectly natural thing to include.

Over time, you may find that the desire to exceed the 3 to 5 article limit is irresistible. A better solution may be to create separate newsletters, perhaps directed at different constituencies within your audience. You can probably even re-use certain components of the newsletters, while better focusing on the needs of disparate segments of your customer base.

4. Sending and follow-up

When you have the newsletter ready, it's time to "pull the trigger" and send it out. Your customer database system may include a facility to do this, or you may need to do it manually. Consult the documentation for your customer database program to learn how you may be able to use it for this purpose.

You may also want to check with your ISP to see if they offer mailing list services. Many ISPs include this in their standard package, and others may be able to provide it for a small fee. Too, there are third-party services such as Topica, Constant Contact, and JangoMail that all supply this capability.

However you send the message, you should set it up so that it is from a monitored email box. If you want to take the time to figure it out, you can usually configure whatever system you use so that error reports go to a different mailbox – this is useful for avoiding having someone's inbox clogged with bounce notices right after you send.

To send the newsletter manually, create a new message, paste your newsletter into the body and subject lines, and then put a chunk of the email addresses into the *blind cc* ("bcc") address. Do *not* make the mistake of including your subscribers' email addresses where they are visible to other subscribers.

You will probably have more addresses than will fit in the bcc box, so you'll probably need to send the message out several times, with a different chunk of addresses in each transmission.

Once the message goes out, there are a couple of things to anticipate. First, you will receive a large number of failure messages. Email addresses change constantly, as people change jobs, change ISPs and even change their names. In addition, unlike the US Postal Service, any typo or other minor error in an email address will doom it to non-delivery.

Be sure that you either correct obvious typos, or remove these addresses from your subscriber list. It's not at all unusual for as much as 20 to 30 percent of even a recently-corrected list of email addresses to fail. In a few cases, the cause may be temporary, but it's probably better to simply unsubscribe failed addresses, rather than re-sending over and over again to dead mailboxes.

Next, no matter how hard you've worked to be sure that people understand that they're signing up to receive email from you, there will inevitably be at least a few nasty responses accusing you of spamming them, and demanding that you remove them from your list.

Do so, and politely reply, confirming that you've removed them. Do not engage in a defensive explanation of why they received the newsletter; that's why you included that information in the newsletter itself. Sadly, many spammers now add text to their messages that claim that the recipient requested the message, so some people can no longer distinguish between a legitimate newsletter and a spam.

Just like any other opportunity for email communication with customers, you should keep a close watch for replies and follow the "acknowledge immediately, answer soon" rule in the course of these conversations as well.

Assessing Results

You can examine your Web site analysis, if you've encouraged readers to visit certain pages. In most cases, you'll see a spike of users entering the site on those pages, and (if it's all worked as intended) a corresponding spike in other activity on your site, as well. As you may expect, this will carry through to increased volumes of leads and information requests, and sales.

What's Next?

As you get a better sense of what content your market considers to be of value, you will be learning what participation they may welcome in an online community. In Project 18, you will learn about newsgroups, and learn how to become a part of these discussions – to the mutual benefit of all involved.

If you're not already analyzing your Web site traffic, it's a good idea to start doing so, in order to measure how well your newsletter is impacting traffic on your site. Project 11 will guide you through the process.

Project 16:
Banner Advertisements

The "golden era" of banner advertising may be over – some contend it never arrived – but there are still opportunities to use this much-maligned advertising medium. Banner ads can be used merely to build brand awareness ("mindshare"), or to draw in very carefully targeted prospects who might not have otherwise known about your company.

Prerequisites

You must have a Web site to promote, and you will be far better able to plan and adjust your banner ad campaigns with effective Web traffic monitoring and analysis. Some graphic-design knowledge will be very helpful.

Cost projections

If you don't do graphic design, you'll want to plan for the expense of finding someone who does. Plan on spending between $250 and $2,500 for each banner, depending on the skill of your artist and the complexity of the banner you create. If you are going to do the work yourself, you know best how long it might take you to build your banners (sometimes referred to as "the creative").

Actually placing the banner ads will probably be your primary expense in this project, though. Budget at least 40 hours' of work to find some good places for your ads, and anywhere from $1,000 on up to cover the advertising costs.

For each banner ad campaign, you should anticipate spending 10 to 20 hours measuring the results and refining the campaign on the basis of the returns you see.

Goals

This is a straightforward marketing activity. As such, the normal measurements of success apply, as seen through the prism of your Web site. Web traffic, lead volume and orders should all be impacted. With a very well targeted ad, you can also expect to see shorter sales cycle/decreased cost of sales, and even larger average order sizes.

Procedures

1. Identifying your targets

Who are the people who buy your products? What sorts of interests do they have? Are there other people who advise or influence your customers? Do these advisors have different interests? How likely are these audiences to browse the Internet? To click on banners? Does your current customer base reflect your ideal customer?

All of these are important questions to ask in deciding whether or not to launch a banner ad campaign. Fortunately, you're likely to have a pretty good sense of the answers to most of them before you even opened this project – most of this is basic market knowledge.

The one question out of these that's liable to be a real stumper is how receptive your target audience is to banner ads. Based on the broad averages on the Internet, less than one-half of one percent of the people who see a given banner ad will click on it. Most sites and brokers sell banner ads in increments of 1,000 "impressions," (quoted as "CPM" – "cost per mega") and you can anticipate less than 5 click-throughs for that many exposures to your ad.

Given that the average CPM in the industry ranges between $20 and $60, that works out more than to $4 to $12 per click-through --- and that's just getting them to your site. Clearly, unless you're selling big-ticket items, you'll have a tough time with the return on investment based solely on click-throughs.

However, there is some value to simple awareness and the "trickle marketing" concept – remind them that you're there and eager to serve. It's been observed that Coca-Cola hardly needs to inform people of what they sell – and yet they spend a fortune on advertising. The payoff, for Coke and for you, is in spurring people to act on their latent needs and desires.

Unfortunately, this is where the crisp accountability that Web-based advertising once promised (through tracking of click-throughs in your Web logs) evaporates, and we sink back into the normal murkiness of measuring the results of any marketing effort. About the only thing you can plan on is noting your overall business results, before and after your banner ad campaign. For most campaigns, you'll probably have to consider any direct Web site results as a bonus.

2. Common banner formats

A banner ad, simply stated, is a graphic device placed on a Web site to fulfill marketing objectives. Banner ads first appeared about ten years ago and have undergone substantial evolution since that time. However, there are a number of standards that have emerged around banner ads.

Most banner ads are either in the GIF ("graphics interchange format") or JPG ("joint picture group") file formats. As a general rule, JPGs are good for static images that require a more photo-realistic appearance. GIF files can include transparent areas and, most important for banner ads, animation, but the image quality is typically lower than that of JPGs.

Some advertisers are experimenting with banner ads that are actually miniature programs. These generally require substantial expertise to produce, however, and are not universally accepted. In some cases, firewalls and other security software will even prevent them from being displayed. Some of the formats that you may hear about in this class of banner ad are Flash and Java.

The most common size is the "classic" 468 pixel ("picture element" – onscreen dot) wide by 60 pixel tall size that you see at the top and bottom of nearly every banner-adorned site on the Web. Other formats are growing in popularity, including "skyscraper" banners that dominate the left or right margins of many pages.

A recent trend, which many Internet users abhor, is the practice of opening a new browser window filled with an oversized banner ad, and either laying it over the content you're trying to view, or sneakily hiding it behind, where you'll come across it later, like litter on your screen. Some advertisers are finding fairly good results with this "pop-up" or "pop-under" format, but there's enough backlash against its users that many advertisers are still giving it a wide berth. Too, most modern browsers simply block such ads entirely, which defeats your purposes if you're using them.

3. Creating the banner

The tools that you use to create a banner ad need to be the ones that you're most comfortable using to manipulate computer graphics. You should have the ability to compress your graphics, as well as to animate them. Fortunately, most of the leading computer graphics tools on the market include all of these capabilities, and you can probably even find specific guidance for using your chosen tool to create banner ads. A quick search with your favorite search engine will probably dig up very useful information.

Research has shown a few common threads behind banner ads that work well. Movement is a very big factor in success – the part of the human brain that processes vision is hard-wired to see movement before nearly anything else. Merely including the words "click here" greatly increases the chance that a viewer will do just that. Like highway billboards, banner ads are taken in at a split-second – so their message needs to be crystal clear at all times, regardless of any animation effects that you may include.

The human eye is also drawn to human faces. If you can include an image of a happy customer, with a clear message in less than five words on how your company changed his or her life for the better, you may have a very effective banner.

Don't build banner ads that mimic in some way the appearance of elements of the operating system or browser of the user – court cases have been fought and lost by advertisers over the misleading nature of these ads. Also, don't build banners that just jump around for the sake of having some eye-catching movement. Unless you've previously found that your target market is susceptible to being irritated into doing business with you, you're unlikely to find that this is the case online.

If you can build three to five different banner ads, you can experiment with them to find the one that works best in each place where you decide to advertise. Most places will allow you to insert multiple ads, and then cull out the weak performers over time.

4. Placement

Where on the Web do your customers browse? Where do they go when they're considering the purchase of a product or service that you offer? These pages are your ideal targets. Sadly, your competitors will already occupy most of them, but you may have the good fortune to be a market leader in your segment.

If your customer base is the general public, nationwide, placing your ad couldn't be easier. You can visit one of the major portals, such as www.yahoo.com, www.msn.com, www.aol.com or www.netscape.com, and simply look for a link leading you to information about advertising. You might also visit one of the leading online advertising agencies, including www.doubleclick.com, which represents dozens of global leaders on the Web.

You should be aware that many of the resources for banner advertisers are focused on mid-sized and large businesses. The small business manager should never consider spending the sort of money that this market does - it can run into the tens or hundreds of thousands of dollars - on *any* form of advertising, let alone putting all of your eggs in the single basket of banner ads. Search carefully for opportunities appropriate to your business, and you're less likely to feel pressured to blow your budget.

If you need to target more closely, many of the sites and agencies that place advertisements can help you with your specific needs. You may spend more per impression, but your overall cost will probably be significantly more within the realm of reality for a small business. National and global advertising is inherently expensive, and may not be appropriate to your needs.

With any of the major sites and agencies, you can usually specify a very narrow interest group you'd like to target. If you know that your organization's ideal customer is a middle-class female, between 22 and 28 years old, preferably in your region, some of the opportunities (notably, DoubleClick) can cater to your needs – for a price, of course.

On directory sites such as www.yahoo.com and www.netscape. com and directory.google.com, you may be able to find a specific page in the directory that you feel will be relevant to your market – and show every visitor there your message.

Another source of outlets that can be very well focused on your specific market segment (and possibly even your geographic range) are the Web sites associated with magazines or other periodicals. Here, you probably won't be able to select within their visitors as much as you could for a major site, but you can sometimes get a great deal of well targeted impressions for not too much money. If you're running print ads in a given periodical, you'll often find that they offer a package that can save you money on both the Web site and on paper.

Microsoft's LinkExchange has some innovative programs that you may want to examine, too. As of this writing, they're guaranteeing a fixed cost per visitor to your Web site, and they have an extensive network of sites on which your ad can appear. Visit their bCentral site at www.bcentral.com for more information.

5. Follow-through and tracking

Placing a banner ad should not be regarded as a "launch and leave" project. In order to ensure that your advertising dollars are being well spent, you must perform some analysis on the results that you get.

The most direct evidence that you can collect will come from click-throughs. For all of their weaknesses as a direct revenue-building tool, the click-throughs prove which banner ads, on which sites, worked the best at getting your prospects' attention. If you find that one banner is out-drawing another, you can usually switch to the stronger performer in mid-course. Of course, you'll want to check on its subsequent performance, to be sure that positive performance on one site doesn't just reflect a peculiarity in its audience.

In order to directly track which banner ad a specific click-through came from, you should set up different entry pages for each ad. They could even have the exact same content (although a tie-in with the ad is not a bad idea), but different names. This way, a quick review of the traffic analysis report will reveal the specific banner and site combination responsible for each and every click-through.

Assessing Results

Using the Web site traffic analyses, you should be able to judge the effectiveness of this form of advertising more immediately than with many other marketing activities. Be careful not to draw firm conclusions from scanty data, though – if you're just running a small test, you may get statistically meaningless data out of it.

Keep an eye on the traditional measures of growing brand aware-ness. Prospects that appear out of nowhere, ready to buy imme-diately with no particular sales effort are a great leading indicator that your market is learning about you. That Web-sourced first order from overseas is another.

What's Next?

With the experience of the most "traditional" of Internet advertis-ing mediums under your belt, you might be curious about the non-traditional opportunities that are out there. Project 17 will guide you through some of the alternatives that you might not have thought of.

Word-of –mouth is the very best sort of marketing, online as in the real world. You can start to build word-of-mouth advertising by carefully using newsgroups, as discussed in Project 18, and by establishing your own customer forum, described in Project 19.

Project 17:
Alternative Internet Advertising

Banner ads and pay-for-placement search engine entries are not
the only opportunities to get the word out on the Internet. In
many cases, you can even inform potential customers about your
organization's products or services by doing a public service
online. As always, the trick is to not offend anyone's advertising-
hostile sensibilities.

Prerequisites

A Web site, email and a strong knowledge of the online resources
that apply specifically to your industry are all necessary for this
project.

Cost projections

If you've already done Project 16, you can re-use the banner ad
creative you built for that effort in parts of this project. You will
probably need to spend 20 to 40 hours looking for and vetting
market-specific online resources, if you haven't already done that.
(This is time well spent anyway.)

The actual costs to place advertisements will vary anywhere from
a nominal donation up to the thousands of dollars per month,
depending on your marketing budget and the quality of the
outlet.

Goals

Identical to the standard marketing activity goals as listed in
Project 16.

Procedures

1. Third-party email newsletters

You may potentially be able to reach a very narrowly targeted audience in third-party email newsletters. As more and more industry email newsletters begin carrying banner ads to defray their expenses, there are many chances to get your message in front of what may be an ideally targeted audience. This is your golden opportunity to do well by doing good.

Be wary of spammers posing as newsletter publishers, however. It's best to stick with newsletters associated with reputable sites. Best of all are email newsletters that you and your customers subscribe to already. If you haven't located any of these, ask a few trusted customers and partners for recommendations.

If the newsletters you find aren't currently featuring any advertisements, you could carefully approach their editors to explore whether this is a matter of policy or of pragmatism. You could even find yourself being asked for advice, and establishing a strong business relationship – one which could serve you very well.

Be aware that the editors of many niche email newsletters are often important analysts and influencers in your market space. By cultivating a good relationship with these people, and by supporting their online outlets, you could be sowing the seeds of a reputation that could pay off with a substantially improved position in the minds of your market leaders.

2. Email list servers

In addition to newsletters, there are many email lists on the Internet. These are somewhat similar to newsgroups (and evolved in parallel with them), but they are delivered into their subscriber's regular email inboxes. If you come across one of these that pertains to your market, again, be aware that this service can cost money to maintain, and its maintainers may be open to a low-key sponsorship message.

Typically, email lists offer the option of receiving every message sent to the list as soon as it's transmitted, or getting the messages in a digest form, either on a periodic (usually daily) or volume basis. If your sponsorship is noted at the bottom of every message, it can serve as a subtle reinforcement that you are a contributing and caring member of the community that forms your market.

You should also strive to make contributions to the discussions on the list. Review Project 18 very closely for guidelines that apply as well here as in newsgroups.

3. Search Engine-Related Advertising

Both Google and Overture offer technology that automatically displays ads relevant to the content on a given page. (You'll sometimes see this on news or blog pages, for example.)

This method of advertising can get your name out there on some of the biggest sites on the Internet, at a very reasonable cost. As with standard search engine advertising (see Project 9), you will pick out key words that will relate the content of a page to an advertisement for your products or services.

Be aware of and adhere to the search engine's content policies, so that you don't suddenly find yourself with no listings because of some minor violation. You will probably set your account up initially through an automated system, and it may only be reviewed by a live person weeks or months later.

Both Google and Overture have programs geared to small businesses, so it behooves you to investigate all of your options closely. You may even want to do test runs with each, to determine where your money is best spent on an ongoing basis.

Assessing Results

You'll measure your results for this project the same way that you did in Project 16.

What's Next?

If you've already learned the lessons of this project, you should go ahead and apply them in the relevant newsgroups, (see Project 18) as well as in email lists. The sense of community is very similar, and there's often overlap between the two.

Project 18:
Using Newsgroups

There are something on the range of 50,000 to 75,000 discussion groups active on the Internet right now. Each of these news-groups is a vibrant community, each with its own unique quirks and rules of etiquette. One wrong word as a business can earn you an electronic black eye in these groups, but well understood and carefully used, they can be one of your most powerful means of communicating with your customers.

Prerequisites

You must have a computer with Internet access, and an email account. Intimate familiarity with proper netiquette can save you a *lot* of trouble (see Project 2).

Cost projections

You may spend as much as 2 to 4 hours initially configuring your system and locating newsgroups relevant to your marketplace. After that, plan to spend at least a few minutes every day, and possibly more than that, if your newsgroups have a large volume of traffic, reviewing the conversations in progress and (eventually) participating in them.

Goals

This project is an exercise in networking, as well as direct market research. You should come away from it with a stronger sense of at least one segment of your marketplace, and you may well find some terrific ideas for new opportunities that your business can seize upon.

1. Understanding newsgroups

First, a brief history lesson. Early in the development of the Internet (and its immediate predecessors), systems were set up that
operated somewhat like a public corkboard. Anyone who wanted
to could post a message, for all to see, or respond to an earlier
message. This development was paralleled on other computer
systems not associated with the nascent Internet, as well.

Over time, this simple concept was refined to include a highly
structured hierarchy of topical groups, moderation (permitting the
manager of a group could decide whether or not a given message
would be posted), and global reach. The modern Usenet ("users'
network") was born in the mid-1980s (from a precursor founded
in 1979) and consisted of a few top-level topical groups, which
were then further broken down into sometimes very narrow
interests. Since then, the number of newsgroups (the individual
discussion groups) has exploded, and there are discussions that
cover nearly any topic you can imagine (and many that you'd
rather not).

When someone posts a message to a newsgroup, it may be held
for moderation, depending on the setup for the specific group. If
the message is approved, or the newsgroup unmoderated, the
message will be sent out to the poster's news server, and then
propagated (retransmitted) until it's available on all of the news
servers that carry that particular newsgroup. From there, anyone
can sign on to their news server and receive all of the messages
posted in that group. News servers typically remove older messages after a certain period of time, or based on the total volume
of messages in the group.

Discussions are organized into "threads," where an initial comment is responded to, then the response may garner its own
responses, and so forth, with the threads sometimes splitting off,
fragmenting, and wandering in ways that can make your head
spin.

2. Gaining access to newsgroups

You have a couple of options here, ranging from the very easy (but less useful) to the somewhat difficult (but very flexible).

The easiest way to get at the majority of the newsgroups out there is to simple visit groups.google.com on the Web. Here, you will have browser-based access to thousands of newsgroups, and you can sign up to get the ability to post from Google, as well.

There are a couple of disadvantages to this approach, though. Most importantly, you don't have an easy way to determine which messages you've already read, and which ones are new. If you're following a particular conversation, the Google Web site doesn't currently give you an easy way to see when new comments have been added. These issues may be addressed in the future as Google enhances their service, but for the moment, they make it difficult to use newsgroups for the purposes of this project.

There are other Web-based means of accessing the Usenet, but they almost universally charge an access fee. This option is designed primarily for those users wishing to gain access to some of the material in newsgroups that is the least likely to be relevant to business uses (i.e., pornography, stolen software and unlicensed music). It's highly unlikely that this is an effective way to spend your firm's money.

The best option is to use a specialized piece of software on your own computer, known as a "newsreader." Most major email packages and browsers include the ability to connect to newsgroups; see the documentation or online help for information about this capability.

At some point as you configure your newsreader, it will ask you to supply the name of a news server. Contact your ISP for this information. If your ISP does not offer a news server, there are a few free servers on the Internet, but they tend to be slow and are often very limited in the range of newsgroups that they carry. Do a search in your favorite search engine on the terms "free news server" or "free nntp server." ("NNTP is "news network transfer protocol" – the common language that different news servers use to transmit and manage newsgroups.)

Alternatively, you can search for a low-cost provider of newsgroup access. If you are willing to exclude access to the "binaries" groups (where files are traded, as mentioned above), you may be able to find a reliable and reasonably inexpensive means of amending your own ISP's inadequate services. Or, you may want to consider switching ISPs.

Once you've configured your newsreader, it will normally give you some way to see which messages you've already read. It will probably also organize the discussion threads for you, and may give you a way to see at a glance when a given newsgroup or thread has received new posts. These capabilities will speed up your daily scan of the newsgroups tremendously, and reduce your frustration with keeping track of the discussions.

3. Finding relevant groups

At this point, one way or another, you have access to the Usenet, and can start to look for those discussion groups that will be of the greatest relevance to your business. Start by searching the newsgroup names for keywords that relate to your products or services. You may even find brand names that you carry, or the names of large competitors.

Broadening your search is something that the groups.google.com site is exceptionally useful for. Simply enter a few search terms that you'd ordinarily use to find information about your products, services, or competitors, and examine the newsgroups that contain hits for your search.

It's also a really sound idea to do a search on your own business name, as well as the names of your principals, just as you did when researching your competitors. You'll get an idea as to how (if) you're regarded by the online communities you're preparing to join.

4. Lurking

This is probably the most important stage of your use of newsgroups. Don't jump right into a newsgroup and start advertising your business. It's usually not even a good idea to immediately start participating in the discussions. The character of each newsgroup is different, and the reactions you get may surprise you, unless you've taken the time to acquaint yourself with the community.

"Lurking" simply means that you watch and observe, without participating. Some newsgroups are rabidly anti-commercial, and speaking out in them will only get you attacked. Others are very laid-back, and commercial participation is eagerly welcomed.

You can also use the groups.google.com site to review the history of many newsgroups, which may give you a chance to accelerate the lurking process. Remember that your goal at this stage of the game is simply to gain a sense of the community that exists in the newsgroup you're studying.

If you come across a conversation where your business is being discussed, particularly in a critical manner, *resist the urge to jump in*, unless there's an explicit comment along the lines of "I just wish that someone at Jones & Co. would explain this to us" – and even then, approach the opportunity with exceptional caution and great calm.

Too many small businesses have earned a reputation for being boorish, defensive and ill tempered by responding before they understood the forum properly. Bear in mind that your comments will be visible to everyone – and will probably remain visible in archives for years. It's almost always better to just let the topic burn out.

5. Flame wars

Nearly every discussion group periodically devolves into a series of acrimonious, sometimes personal attacks. When this happens, tempers flare, feelings get hurt, and reputations can be shattered forever. This is called a flame war.

Do not participate in flame wars.

If a message of yours inadvertently started the ball rolling, it *might* be reasonable to quietly apologize for starting the fracas, and then lay low until it dies down. Just as with individual emails, you should always re-read your message before you send it. Watch for anger in your tone, even if unintended.

If you find that your organization is the subject of a flame war, you *must* resist the urge to participate. Nearly without exception, you will make matters worse, and end up damaging your reputation in the group.

Keep your head down, and watch for any opportunities to improve the way you do business, so that there will be no basis for a flame war in the future. There may a kernel of truth in the painful, sometimes even slanderous comments that you see. Take advantage of the candidness of the conversation to look for these nuggets.

6. Making contributions

As you become familiar with the members of a discussion group, you may come to feel that you know them, and that you'd like to help solve their problems and answer their questions. This is a natural part of joining an online community, and you can do your business a lot of good by becoming a trusted resource there.

However, it's very rarely appropriate to flog one of your products or services as the answer to a member's issue. At the most, you can consider mentioning it in passing, but even that may rub some groups the wrong way. Watch for precedents as you lurk, and watch the reactions of the group.

Some groups have well-established norms for commercial partici-pation – putting a note in the subject line, or otherwise flagging a biased opinion – and others have no tolerance for it. However, in most groups, it's perfectly acceptable to include your business name and URL in your signature block.

Over the long run, if members of the community see that your business is associated with useful answers, insightful commentary and unfailing politeness, they will tend to want to do business with you, and to send their friends, too.

7. Tilt the playing field

When someone in the discussion group asks for a referral, or a recommendation for a business to help them with something, you want to be sure that your name comes up. The best way to do that is to make it very easy for your happy customers to participate in the group.

This is a method that may take a while to show results, but the impact can be long lasting and exceptionally powerful. It is also entirely dependent on you serving your customers well enough that they want to recommend that other people do business with you. The worst possible case is that you successfully get a number of your customers into the group, and they proceed to warn prospects away.

If you've found a particularly useful newsgroup, you can tell your customers about it. Better yet, let them jump right onto it. You can include a link on your Web site that a correctly configured newsreader will follow right to the group. (E.g., "news:rec.crafts. brewing.") (For mailing list discussion groups, you can supply a form on your Web site that permits them to simply enter their email address and subscribe immediately.)

By stacking the deck this way, you're not only building the opportunity to have a rich source of referrals, but you're also doing your customers a service, by directing them to a resource on the Internet that will be useful to them.

Assessing Results

The primary returns from this project will be your own greater knowledge of your marketplace, as well as exposure to a global community. Watch for referrals from the discussion groups, and be alert for lessons that you can learn from any criticisms voiced – about your business, or about your competitors.

What's Next?

You may have found that there just aren't any discussion groups that are particularly relevant to your marketplace. If this is the case, then you may want to consider doing Project 19, where you will set up a forum for your customers to meet and talk online.

Project 19:
Creating a Customer Forum

The public newsgroups may be too raucous a place for your customers to gather and exchange information. Or, you may want to provide a private place for them to air their grievances and give input on your plans. Whatever the case may be, a customer forum can be a fascinating exercise – and one that is guaranteed to surprise you.

Prerequisites

In order to begin this project, you need a personal computer with an Internet connection, and an email account.

Cost projections

Since the majority of the services that enable you to establish a customer forum are supported by advertisements, your primary expense for this project will probably be your time. If you would prefer to do away with the advertisements, you may need to spend some money on a list server provider – figure between $5 and $40 per month to start. This cost may rise as the volume of messages and number of subscribers increase.

Goals

A customer forum can serve a number of different goals. You may simply use it to mine your customer base for idea. It may turn into a source of referrals, or your existing customers may even push prospects along to close sales. As your customers help each other out, you may also see reduced support expenses.

1. Technology and hosting options

As usual, you have a number of options to choose from when you're setting up a customer forum. Some are exceptionally simple, but very powerful, and others are fairly complex, with their own benefits.

Probably the easiest option to use is to set up an email list with a service like groups.yahoo.com or groups.google.com. These providers can get you started immediately, at no cost, and with a good deal of flexibility in managing the subscriber base and the messages. Most offer the ability to view messages via a Web interface, including an archive of old messages.

The main drawback to these services is that most of them insert advertising in the messages that are sent to your customers. It's usually better if any promotional messages they see in association with your organization are about your organization.

To get similar services, but without the advertisements, you can go to a provider such as www.biglist.com, or www.listbox. com. For a relatively small fee, usually under $50 per month for a small number of subscribers, they will host your mailing list. You'll have complete control over the list, and have no ads on the messages, other than any that you choose to insert yourself. (Note that these services may also be useful for sending your email newsletter, established in Project 15.)

If your mail server supports it, you could even set up a private newsgroup. This may be an intriguing option to pursue, as it offers many of the benefits of newsgroups (see Project 17), while giving you total control. See the documentation and online help for your server, to learn whether it supports this capability, and how to exploit it.

Your ISP may also include email discussion lists in your package, or as a low-cost add on. Note that this is very similar to, and may even be the same as, the systems that you would use to send newsletters, as described in Project 15. The difference is that now, you're going to be allowing anyone on the list send messages to the whole group.

2. Drawing an audience

If you have an established email newsletter, you can promote the existence of your new customer forum heavily there. Of course, the part of your Web site focused on current customers is another good place to take note of the new service to your market.

You will need to consider whether or not to permit non-customers to take part in the forum. There are advantages and disadvantages – a large group of satisfied customers is a powerful sales tool, but it can be good to have a private place to air dirty laundry. Of course, you can have it both ways, by simply establishing two forums, but this may diminish the value of each.

If you do decide to throw open the doors, be sure to tell prospects about the forum. Encourage them to use it as a resource to get (reasonably) unbiased and unscripted answers to any questions that they may have.

3. Responding to negatives

As a matter of course, you should keep a close eye on the activity in any forum where your customers and prospects are gathered. One that you've established is no different. Unlike newsgroups or email lists that other people run, it is appropriate for you to respond to most negative comments that are made on your own forum.

However, the same rules regarding inflammatory responses still apply here. If a customer or prospect sees that you respond calmly and positively to complaints that are aired in your customer forum, it will only improve their opinion of you, almost without any regard for the seriousness of the original complaint.

Remember that most people are unlikely to complain when something bothers them. Instead, they'll take their business elsewhere, and quietly advise their friends to do likewise. Someone who's taken the time to state a grievance is giving you a terrific opportunity to not only set things right for them, but also to demonstrate publicly that you are committed to doing so for any unhappy customer.

If the discussion turns into a flame war, it's your responsibility as the forum owner to try to restore order. Strive to avoid even the appearance of chastising participants in a conflagration on the basis of their support of or opposition to your business, if it's the topic of the discussion. Remind the group what the purpose of the forum is, and point out how the current argument runs counter to that purpose.

4. Drawing on the resource

As your customers (and, potentially, prospects) become comfortable with discussing your products and services in an open and honest forum, you can learn a great deal from them. You can use the customer forum as a sounding board for ideas that you are considering for future offerings.

Your customers may also share innovative ways that they're getting the most out of your business. You may find great opportunities through these discussions for new ways to enhance the revenue that your products and services bring in, or you may find that your market has a different perception of their value than you do.

The forum can serve as an early warning system for problems that might have taken months to show up in formal business metrics. A pattern of complaints might uncover weaknesses in your organization. Seeing your customers routinely heap praise on a specific employee might serve as notice that a promotion or raise is in order.

Most of all, though, as your customers develop a community that's based around their business relationship with your organization, it will give them yet one more reason to continue doing business with you.

Assessing Results

As your customers help each other, post-sales support costs may decline, as well as pre-sales support. You may gain insights that allow you to optimize your pricing model. Finally, the increases in customer loyalty will help to improve repeat business and retention.

What's Next?

Continue to monitor and participate in the conversations you've started in your marketplace. Look for other opportunities to directly interact with your customers. If you have not already done so, follow Project 17 to find newsgroups and other public forums where your customers are building communities.

Project 20:
Automated Lead Entry

Giving your prospects the opportunity to contact you directly from your Web site can be a great use of the technology. However, it's all too easy for this to become burdensome, and an opportunity for human error to creep in. There's no need to take that risk, when you can get the computer to do the dull parts of the job.

Prerequisites

You must have a Web site and email. You should also have experience with creating Web-based forms (Project 14), and you must have some form of lead management or customer relationship management (CRM) software.

Cost projections

Depending on the complexity and flexibility of the email interface into your lead management or CRM system, this project will take between 2 and 4 weeks of your time to fully implement. If you decide to bring someone in to perform the work, budget from $5,000 to $40,000 for a skilled CRM consultant to do the job.

Goals

By completing this project, you will be able to more quickly respond to leads that come from your Web site. You will also reduce the potential for errors in processing them. Companies that respond quickly to leads that come from the Internet, in particular, are more likely to have a chance to proceed through the rest of the process to the sale.

Procedures

1. Building a Web form

Drawing on your experience in Project 14, you should create a form that requires the information that you'll need in order to respond to the lead. Typically, this will include the visitor's name, email address, phone number, and physical address. If you sell exclusively to businesses, you can also require the business name.

Beware of presenting the visitor with a lengthy page of required fields – many Web users are wary of providing very much information at all, and may balk at a large number of questions. Your best bet will be to just ask for the minimum information that you need in order to determine who should contact the prospect, and how to contact them. Once you have established human contact, you can always gather the additional information you need – whereas if they decide to just skip it because you're asking too many questions, you'll never regain that opportunity.

Be sure, too, that you prominently post a privacy statement of some sort. Again, a visit to www.truste.com is well worth your time, and it is probably worthwhile to complete the necessary steps to display the TRUSTe seal.

If you may be collecting information from children under 13, there are special legal considerations. Accepting personal data from children must be done in compliance with COPPA (Children's Online Privacy Protection Act), which raises very stringent barriers to providing services online that cater to children, requiring direct and verifiable parental consent for the collection of any personally-identifiable data.

The European Union also has very strict rules regarding what you may and may not do with data you collect from their citizens. As well, the United States has some new laws that apply to any data received from credit reporting agencies. Consult your lawyer for guidance as to how you can comply with these requirements.

In any event, you should be aware that if your privacy statement commits you to not share with third parties the data that you collect from your customers online, you must abide by that commitment, or face legal action. If you do not make such a commitment, you may get fewer leads via your Web site.

Once you create the form itself, you'll have a couple of choices as to how to move the data it collects from your Web server into your lead management tool. In most cases, email will be the most dependable method, though it does present security concerns. Build the email so that it is formatted in a predictable way so that the receiving system can easily identify which part of the message represents which piece of data.

More technologically advanced means, such as directly recording the data into your internal database may offer some advantages, but they are more difficult to build. In addition, giving the Web server the ability to access an internal database for this purpose means that, should your Web server be compromised at some point in the future, the hacker may also have access to your database.

You can also write the data to a separate database, and then check that database periodically for new information. This can be the simplest method, and is likely to be a bit more secure than email, but it will probably slow down your response time substantially.

Whichever of these you choose, the page that displays after the visitor sends his or her information in to you should include links to further information about your products or services, as well as sincere thanks for their interest. You should also set the expectation for what and when the next step will be. If you will call the prospect within one business day, say so. If you'll send information immediately, let the visitor know what to expect in the mail.

2. Linking to the back end

Your lead management or CRM system runs on some form of a database. It's unlikely that you will want to take the leads that come from the Web site and just put them directly into the database. You'll want to have a human at least look at them, screen them for duplication of existing records, and also make a quick judgement as to their validity.

The best approach, given this, is to build a means of temporarily storing the lead, and then having someone screen it and then import it into the system. Modern CRM systems will probably have some facility for accomplishing this built in. If not, you may need to build something to enable this capability.

Ideally, you will have the ability to screen and import the leads from the Web in nearly real time -- nothing impresses a prospect as much as receiving an email or telephoned acknowledgement of his or her inquiry within minutes – better yet, while they're still on your site! This requires a good deal of commitment to managing the Web lead process, though, and it may not be worth the resources.

However, at a bare minimum, there should be some form of immediate acknowledgement that the lead information has arrived. You may even want to have the process on your Web site that handles the form generate this acknowledgement email. Be aware, though, that if something goes wrong between where the form is submitted and where you respond to the prospect, this can lead to great misunderstandings, and lost sales opportunities.

Assessing Results

The ability to respond more quickly to prospective customers' inquiries on the Web will set the pace for the overall speed of the sales process. With a shorter sales cycle, your cost of sales will drop, and your sales staff can make more sales with the same resources, which both reduces expenses and raises revenues. In addition, by reducing the opportunity for error, you can avoid missing out on good opportunities for bad reasons.

What's Next?

With the experience of capturing detailed prospect data under your belt, you might want to start applying similar methods to your support tasks, in Project 21. Now that your site is a direct lead generation tool, you should also ensure that you're doing what you can to drive traffic to it. Projects 16 and 17 go through some powerful strategies to accomplish this.

Project 21:
Customer Self-Help

Imagine being able to answer most customer questions anytime, day or night. You can make your customers and prospects happier, as well as reducing the number of late-night panicked calls you have to handle, by enabling a few simple self-help tools on your Web site.

Prerequisites

You must have a Web site. Your support knowledge base should be in an electronic format, and you'll benefit from having an "always on" Internet connection.

Cost projections

Building and posting an electronic version of your FAQ ("frequently asked questions") listing will probably take around 4 to 8 hours; maintaining it may take as much as an hour a month. If you have not developed HTML skills in-house, you should probably budget between $250 and $500 to have the document added to your Web site.

Enabling customer access to an electronic knowledge base will probably be a task for your Web resource; if this is a consultant, budget somewhere between $5,000 and $15,000 to have it set up with a maintenance procedure that you can manage yourself.

Goals

The rewards for a successful customer self-service initiative are tremendous. Many organizations with effective online tools for their customers' use find that the Web site itself becomes a selling point for their products or services. Customer retention, repeat sales and referrals will all increase, while your support costs will drop.

Procedures

1. Just the FAQs

A "Frequently Asked Questions" listing is a very easy tool to provide, and, as its name implies, it will handle the most common issues your customers face, at little or no additional cost to you.

If your support organization doesn't already have a document that covers the daily repeat questions, have them keep a tally for a few days or a week. Phrase the questions in a clear, concise manner, trying to ask them the way that the customers do. For example, if your customers will refer to a part by number, then it's fine for you to do so, too. However, if they'll more likely call it "the blue plastic piece," then it's probably more appropriate for you to do the same.

Write the answers with the same goal of clarity from the customers' point of view. A step-by-step approach works well, as does a "symptom, cause, solution" format. Once you've got a draft of the FAQ, use it with real customers for a week or two. Make any changes that appear to be necessary, and then post it on your Web site.

At least once a month, you should review the FAQ listing to see whether the answers need revision, and to add any new questions that have become common enough to warrant inclusion. Of course, if you have a new product line, a substantial change in your business or any other event for which you can foresee getting a lot of phone calls and emails, you can prepare a special-purpose FAQ just for the occasion.

2. Enabling customers to search for answers

If you have an extensive knowledge base already established in electronic form, then you know how useful it is to your customer support staff. Extending that useful information to the Internet is an important part of an overall Internet self-support strategy. If your support needs are simple enough that you have not yet put together a resource like this for your staff, then you can move on to the next step in this project.

The process that we'll follow in this part of the project will be to convert the content into HTML documents (one per question-and-answer), publish them to your Web site, create a search page and finally, establish a process for keeping this content up-to-date.

Getting your knowledge base into HTML documents may be a relatively easy process, depending upon the tools that you're using to manage it already. If you're using one of the major support automation packages, you may find that it already has the ability to export the knowledge base as HTML. Check the documentation and online help for guidance as to whether this is the case.

If your support automation product does not allow you to export into HTML, look for options allowing you to export into other formats. Failing that, you may have to go and find where the content is stored yourself. If you've had someone else doing the implementation and management of your support automation system for you, you'll probably have to bring him or her in to do this for you.

If you've been maintaining your knowledge base in a word-processing document, any modern word processor will let you export into HTML; it's just a matter of breaking up the content into one file per answer. Indeed, nearly any modern software package with which you may have been managing your knowledge base will generate HTML documents. Again, consult documentation or help files for more information.

If you have not been maintaining your knowledge base in any electronic format, and you still want to make this knowledge available to your customers via your Web site, you'll need to have someone turn it into electronic documents, and produce HTML files from them.

As you produce these HTML documents, you should resist the urge to place a lot of formatting and navigation material on them.

Some form of search engine software will index them, and extraneous material on the pages can cause the tools great confusion.

Just as with the FAQs, you'll need to ensure that the language and terminology is appropriate to your customer base. To use the same example, your customer support analysts may well know parts by their part number, and so when a given part number is given in the knowledge base, they can proceed to describe the part to the customer. In this case, you may want to supply both the part number and a parenthetical customer-friendly description of it.

The same will apply to a wide range of situations where you have internal jargon that's completely understood so long as the audience is within your four walls, but will serve only to deepen the customer's confusion. Ensure, too, that the spelling and grammar are checked over carefully, just as on the rest of your site.

Move the documents up to your Web site, ideally placing them in a separate folder for manageability. At this point, even without a search engine to allow your customers to find their answers via your Web site, you can start to provide links in reply emails, directing customers to this answer or that, rather than having to paste the entire answer into each message. Of course, you should only use this method with those customers who have good Web access.

As you prepare to create a search page on your site, there are a few considerations to keep in mind. First and foremost, as always, must be usability. Your search pages should retain the look and feel of the rest of your site. Remember that the answer pages must be relatively unadorned, in order to avoid confusing the software that will search them. You may need to use one of a variety of techniques that allow you to embed dynamic content like this inside a static context. Consult your Web expert or HTML design books for more information.

This brings us to the matter of the tool that you'll use to enable searching. Depending upon what Web server you're using, you have a number of options here. There are certainly very powerful third-party systems, including offerings from most of the major

Web search engines. The advantage of these is that you have relatively little maintenance to do, and someone else is responsible for the care and feeding of the technology. Some of the options even come at little or no expense.

However, if you'd like to minimize expenses and maintain full control over the process, there are many options that you can run on your own systems. For a comprehensive listing of the available search tools, as well as links to reviews and tips about using them, see www.searchtools.com. This site also includes examples of many third-party systems, so you can get a sense of how these might work for you.

Search engines are a relatively complex Web technology, and so you may wish to bring in an expert to help you with the selection and implementation of the tool that you choose.

When you have the system functional, you should consider whether it should be available to all Web site visitors, or whether you want to secure it somehow. There are benefits and risks to both approaches. While it can be worrisome to have sensitive information –potentially uncovering flaws in your products or services – posted where anyone can see them, a customer who needs an answer *now* may be more than disappointed at being denied access to the solution for lack of a password.

A balanced approach might be to leave the knowledge base open to all comers, but remove those answers that you would prefer your competitors never see. This may somewhat compromise the usefulness of the content, but it at least leaves it available. Substituting an irate late-night call from someone looking for a solution with one from someone looking for a password may not be a very satisfying outcome.

Once you've got a knowledge base search capability up and running on your site, the final thing that you must do is to ensure that the content remains current and accurate. If your knowledge base remains relatively static, you can probably just ensure that the process of accomplishing any changes to it now includes making the changes on the Web content, as well.

If you have a very fluid knowledge base, however, you should probably think about a periodic process of re-publishing to the Web. Again, if your knowledge base management tool permits export as HTML, it may also include a facility to publish changes automatically.

A good practice is to simply remove all of the content and copy a fresh version of it every so often. The frequency of re-publishing will depend entirely upon how often major changes are made to your knowledge base, but once a week is pretty typical. Of course, if you discover a substantial error, you should always correct it as soon as possible.

If you can incorporate a feedback capability into your published knowledge base pages, you can then use that information to improve weak pages and to consider giving more prominence to strong ones in customers' search results.

Once your customers can research their issues on your Web site, your support staff will probably see a couple of trends. The questions that come in will probably become more difficult – the Web site will start to catch most of the easy ones – and the overall volume may drop, allowing the staff to focus on solving those more difficult questions.

3. Taking questions online

The first stage of this project is to simply ensure that your customer support email address is plastered across all of the support-related portions of your Web site, as well as appearing on the contact information page, and possibly even on the home page. You should have already done this, as part of the basic Web site design, but ensure that it's included on each of the FAQ and knowledge base search pages, as well.

If you have a support staff of more than one, it's a good idea to set up a generic support email address, and then ensure that this address is closely monitored. Your support automation system may even give you a way to automatically monitor this address, and put the messages received there directly into the system. Have a look at the documentation for information on this capability.

To take this concept to the next level, a natural extension of Project 14, where you accepted generic feedback from your customers, is to create a specialized support-request form. Ensure that any information that you must have in order to respond to a support request is required on the form, and, again, make sure that it's directed to the generic support email address. Of course, the form can also encourage them to try out the self-help tools you've established, with easy links to the FAQ and knowledge base search pages.

When you used online support tools in Project 5, you will remember that some organizations use automated systems that reply with potential answers. In general, the expense of these systems is well beyond what a small business can support. In addition, they typically require a large amount of maintenance and planning, overhead that's only justifiable for very large support organizations.

4. Follow-through

When you receive requests for support via email, ensure that whatever system or team that receives these messages gives an immediate acknowledgement, together with any tracking number that may apply to the request.

You need to ensure that they are given a priority within your support organization. Remember that having your customers communicate with you via email is something that you want to encourage. The costs to your organization are reduced, and the quality of the communication is generally increased. If they learn that they consistently get good, well-researched answers by using email, they're more likely to continue doing so.

Just as through any medium, your support staff may receive messages that are irate or abusive. Remind your staff that, whether or not the customer's anger is justified, the only proper response to it is calm and rational, focusing on solving the problem, rather than on the customer's emotional reaction to it. Remember that the process of sitting in front of an impersonal computer screen seems to make people feel that it's more appropriate to vent rage than they might typically do with a live human voice or face to relate to.

Remember the truism that customers are always expecting more – the best service experience they've ever had sets the new benchmark for the minimum that they'll expect in the future. If you can set that benchmark, you will make it all the more difficult for your competitors to impress your customers.

Assessing Results

As mentioned, your support staff may find that, though their calls are more infrequent, they're becoming more complex. Further, you will likely find that you can serve a larger customer base with the same size support staff, allowing you to defer new hires. The results associated with increased customer loyalty will also apply here.

What's Next?

With your increased awareness of the potential for online support tools, you may want to go back to Project 5, and refine your use of the Internet to solve your own issues with the products and services you use. As you do so, you will probably see features and approaches that you'd like to incorporate into your own tools.

Project 22:
Online Catalogue

If you have a broad inventory of products to offer, particularly if that inventory changes frequently, maintaining current and accurate information on your Web site may seem like an administrative nightmare. However, it need be no more burdensome than managing your inventory in a database.

Even better, when you can accurately communicate the state of your inventory to your customers, they will be more confident that you can fulfill their requests – or at least have a solid idea of what to expect. Setting accurate expectations is a key ingredient to great customer relationships.

Prerequisites

You must have a Web site, preferably one hosted at your location. You must also maintain some form of inventory database in a timely fashion.

Cost projections

Expect to spend between 4 and 6 weeks on the initial setup, or between $10,000 and $20,000 if you have a consultant do it for you.

Goals

Imagine how much more smoothly your business will run when customers order only what you can provide, or at least have a good understanding of what the timeframes for delivery will be. You'll have fewer complaints, a better reputation, and perhaps even increased sales, as customers see that an item they're torn about is low in stock.

Procedures

1. Identifying a data source

You may have a business where the products you sell are created only upon demand. Or, you may be selling services, where only the resources of your staff limit the supply. If these cases apply to you, then this project is significantly easier.

However, if you maintain stock, and need to ensure that your customers can see at a glance whether a given item can be supplied immediately, or will have a delay on it, this project will offer you the means to implement this very powerful capability.

Either way, you must have some sort of a data source today, which will serve to populate your catalogue. For a static catalogue (where you don't need to display stocking levels), you can just use your existing product lists.

If you have a formal inventory system (or even an informal one, such as a cash register software package), this is an obvious data source, although you'll need to ensure that it's being kept current in order to extract the maximum value from this project. You should find out how you can get access to its database, consulting the documentation and online help.

Then, you'll need to decide whether you want to update the information in the online catalogue instantly when you make a sale, or whether you'd prefer to do it on a periodic scheduled basis. Instant updates will give you greater assurance that your site accurately reflects your product availability, but can be quite a lot more complex to implement.

2. Establishing a format

It's a good practice to establish a template for your product catalogue detail pages. This will make putting the data in much easier, and will enable you to centralize changes that you need to make. The template should draw on the look and feel that you've established for the rest of your site.

As always, the watchword with your catalogue pages must be usability. If you have multiple families of products, it should be easy to navigate between and within them. Some of your products may have natural add-ons; if this is the case, you should include links right to the add-ons – it will drive sales of those items.

If your product is one that customers are used to looking at before they purchase, make sure that you plan for photos and diagrams of the product. Think about how customers examine the products – for example, if you're selling apparel, make sure that your photos include the details that customers examine in person – stitching, fabric weave and so forth.

If you're selling a highly technical product, be sure that you include links to all of the relevant technical data – though you may not want to include all of the details on the product page itself.

If you sell products with closely related variants (such as size or color), you should think about whether you need to have a separate catalogue page for each variant, or whether you should simply plan to display the availability of each on one master page for the product itself.

3. Setting expectations

It may be appropriate for you to plan to show the exact stock level of each product in your catalogue. However, if the thought of that level of detail about your state of business being publicly available worries you, then you can simply indicate that a product with sufficient quantities in stock is available immediately.

Defining what's sufficient stock level to make a commitment of immediate availability will depend upon your knowledge of how quickly the given item may sell. Particularly if you're going to be updating periodically (as opposed to constantly), you need to determine how many of a given item you must have in stock in order to say that it will be available with a reasonable level of assurance.

If an item is out of stock, or will be produced upon demand, you should give the customer an idea of how long it will take to fulfill an order for it. This way, you head off the inevitable questions, and are still able to capture the business. Be very conservative when settling on a timeframe to share with the customer. Most people will understand if there's going to be a delay in filling their request. However, if you promise 4 to 6 weeks, and often take 8 to 10 weeks, you will damage your reputation for being honest about product availability.

This is particularly critical in businesses where time-sensitive sales are common. If you sell products that are often given as gifts, you must be sure to tell customers accurately how much lead time you'll need. An IOU on Christmas morning is a black eye for your business name.

As you incorporate catalogue content into your Web site, you should also be sure to indicate any limitations that may exist on your ability to serve certain geographic areas or other customer segments. A customer who places an order on your site that you can't or won't fill is doing you no good at all, so set these expectations right up front, too.

4. Publishing the catalogue

Now that you've laid out what the format will be, and selected a data source, you can start putting the two together. If you're enabling real-time inventory, you will be best served to build the actual catalogue pages so that they are data driven.

In other words, instead of ordinary HTML pages in a directory on your Web server's hard drive, your catalogue pages would be created only when a user requests them, and would include data drawn directly from your chosen data source.

If your site is hosted at your facility, this should be much easier than if it's hosted at your ISP's office. If you're still hosting your site on someone else's servers, you may find it difficult or impossible to achieve this level of currency in your catalogue pages.

If you went through Project 14, you have some familiarity already with scripting. Creating dynamic pages, driven by your inventory data, is a task that nearly all scripting technologies will also be capable of. If you can create dynamic pages, this will also make it much easier for you to effect changes that need to impact all of the pages in your catalogue – or on your site.

Security will be very important, if you're permitting live access from your Web server into your internal database. If possible, you should configure your firewall so that the only access permitted is by the specific scripts that generate your catalogue pages, and you must ensure that you use secure user names and passwords for all systems involved. It's more critical than ever that you keep an active eye on security updates for all of your systems, as well.

If you decide to generate static pages instead, do try to find some way to do it in a similar fashion – in other words, create your static pages automatically. You can usually accomplish this by setting up a process that pushes your catalogue data into templates, generating new pages for each item.

One advantage of static page generation is that you can accomplish it with much greater security. You can run the generation process within your firewall, and then post the resulting pages up through the same means that you would publish any other new Web content.

Another advantage is that search engines will be able to much more easily index your catalog content. Given that there are a number of specialized search engines now appearing that are focused on searching online catalogs and giving customers a comparative listing, this can be an important source of new business.

Be sure to look into the opportunities to provide a data feed to some of these search engines. Google's www.froogle.com, in particular, welcomes catalogue data in a formatted, periodic upload, and will list your products for all the world to find. See their Web site for details.

5. Refreshing the catalogue

If you're running dynamic catalogue pages, the only thing you need worry about is making sure that the underlying data source is kept current. If that's based on your existing inventory database, this is as simple as ensuring that this system is used faithfully.

If you are generating static pages, you may want to see whether you can automate that process. Once automated, you can run it much more frequently – which will help to maintain the currency of the catalogue.

It's important that any changes in any of the information that you publish be made as soon as possible. Pricing changes, specification updates, availability and so forth should all be kept current. This applies to any search engine data feeds that you may be providing as well.

Assessing Results

By making your catalogue available online, you will likely drive sales, as your prospects can see exactly what you're offering. In addition, you can greatly increase your market reach, by making your offerings visible anytime, to anyone, anywhere in the world.

What's Next?

Once you have your products detailed on your Web site, the next obvious step is to be able to accept orders right on your site. Learn how in Project 23.

Project 23:
Advanced E-commerce

The next logical step beyond an online catalogue is to put those items on sale. There are a wide variety of approaches to this bold step into the online world. Some don't require very much risk, and are not hard to implement. Others are a little harder, but offer you better control over the process.

The biggest hurdle is managing payment arrangements. This project assumes that you will want to take credit cards. If your products or services don't lend themselves to this approach, this project is worth reading anyway, since it covers some of the basics of taking customer orders on the Web, as well.

Prerequisites

You must have a Web site, and you'll need to have the ability to run specialized software on your Web server. Typically, this will mean that you have your own server, either located at your ISP's site, or at your own offices.

You will either need to have completed Project 22 to create your online catalogue, or at least have done some of the steps in it, so that you have an up-to-date listing of your products (and, potentially stocking levels).

Cost projections

Development or acquisition and installation of a shopping cart application may cost you in the range of $1,000 to $15,000. You may also have expenses relating to credit card processing, typically between 1% and 3% of your gross online sales. An SSL certificate, necessary to provide for secure transmission of financial data from your customers, will probably cost around $75 to $200 per year.

If you do not already have a full-blown firewall to protect your data and your customers' information, you'll need to budget between $20,000 and $100,000 to select, install, and configure one.

Goals

The largest goal that this project should allow you to meet is increasing your overall sales volume. Usually, this means that you will be able to achieve lower cost of sales, and thereby increase your overall profitability.

By setting up your own e-commerce system, you will have better control over the sales process, and you'll be able to integrate your online sales efforts with the rest of your business systems. This should permit you to perform better analysis and forecasting, which will improve your ability to react to shifts in market conditions.

Procedures

1. Accepting payment online

If you already accept credit card payments in your business, you can probably process online orders through your existing systems. Check with your financial institution for any terms or conditions that they may apply to such use.

Many businesses accept their online customers' credit card information online, and then simply process the charge through their existing offline systems. This can be a low-cost and secure approach; just be sure that you clear any electronic record of your customers' credit card data once you've processed their order, to keep it from attracting hackers.

If you have not yet started to accept credit cards, then there are some reasonably priced options on the market for you. eBay's PayPal is a market leader in this space, and does not require a huge amount of setup or configuration in order to integrate its system into your Web site. See www.paypal.com for more information.

There are other providers in this space – a quick look on your favorite search engine for "credit card processing" will bring up a number of links. You should also check with your financial institution to see what they offer.

You can also simply have your customers call you to give their credit card information, assuming that you have a card-processing machine in your business already. This allows you to bypass Step 2 in this project, as you will not need to manage secure transmission of this data.

If you need to retain complete control over credit card processing, and want to accomplish it online, you'll need to coordinate several systems in your Web site. First, you'll have to set up a secured Web page, to prevent hackers from intercepting this sensitive data as it moves between your customer's computer and yours.

Next, you'll have to transmit the request (again, securely) to a processing service, which will handle confirming funds and actually crediting them to your account. Typically, this process will return a confirmation number for each transaction. At this point, you can fulfill the order, relatively secure in the knowledge that payment is confirmed.

2. Fraud

Unfortunately, the anonymity of the Internet does enable rip-off artists to ply their trade with relative ease. When a thief gets a stolen credit card number, it's not uncommon for an online shopping spree to follow.

If you're unfortunate enough to be one of the merchants the thieves choose to patronize, you may end up having to take a chargeback, and be out the merchandise, plus any chargeback fees. In addition, if you get a reputation as being a "safe" place to use stolen credit cards, there could be more serious repercussions, including legal action.

Fortunately, most credit card processing services have some fraud-prevention systems built into their offerings. Commonly, they'll verify that the shipping address matches the billing address, or that the billing address given by the customer matches that on record with the card issuer. Some more sophisticated systems even look for patterns of purchase that look fraudulent.

Discuss with your processing service what fraud-prevention services they offer, and use this as a criterion for selecting a new provider if the answers are not to your satisfaction.

3. Setting up a secure page

If you will be taking credit cards on your site, you must provide a secure page from which they may be transmitted. The open nature of the Internet means that most traffic that flows across the public networks can be directly examined and decoded, unless it's been protected with strong encryption prior to transmission.

Encryption of a Web-based transaction is usually accomplished through SSL ("secure sockets layer"). This requires that you have an SSL certificate installed, which is simply an electronic document that uniquely identifies your business. It certifies that you have provided proof of your business name, domain name, and location to a trusted third-party issuer.

With an SSL certificate, your Web server can then encrypt the information it transmits with your customer's computer. This is also the process that causes the customer's browser to display a "lock" icon, as described in Project 4. The encryption scrambles the data being sent well enough that a hacker will be unable to practically get at the information.

To learn about getting an SSL certificate, you can visit www.verisign.com, www.thawte.com, or www.geotrust.com. Although there are other vendors of SSL certificates, you may experience problems with your certificate being recognized by some browsers if a minor player in this market issues it. These "certificate authorities," as they are known, are recognized as trustworthy by nearly all browsers.

Typically, you will need to get your Web server to generate a request document, which includes your business information and a unique key (a string of data unique to that machine). This document is then submitted to a certificate authority, who will then return a completed certificate authorization to you. Follow the directions given by the certificate authority and your Web server manufacturer to complete installation of the SSL certificate.

With the certificate installed, you should now be able to launch a secure page in your test browser by simply replacing the normal "http" at the head of your Web address with "https." You should see the SSL icon in your browser, and be able to click on it to view the details of your certificate.

4. Security is more critical than ever

Before you launch into e-commerce, the worst that could happen if your systems got hacked was disruption of your business, destruction of electronic records, and the inconvenience of recovery. (Gee, is that all?)

Now, though, the stakes are quite a bit higher. If a hacker compromises the systems where you process and store customers' credit-card information, you could inadvertently leave the door open for a hacker to steal their credit cards. It's not inconceivable that you could be held liable for their losses, in addition to all of the consequences mentioned above.

You've probably even heard of major e-commerce sites where the servers containing credit card data were hacked. It's worth noting that some of these companies are no longer with us.

So, what to do about it? If you haven't previously done so, now is the time to invest in an industrial-strength firewall for your business. Firewalls can either react to known types of attacks, or to activity that looks generally suspicious. Those that deal with known attacks may permit a brand-new type of attack to slip by; the more proactive firewalls may block some legitimate activities. You will need to make your selection based on your own level of concern.

As you evaluate different firewall vendors, keep in mind that this is an industry where paranoia is a normal state of being, and where there is sometimes some difficulty in striking the appropriate balance between security and workability. Try not to end up with a system that's so secure that nobody can - or will- use it. It's been observed that the security consultant's idea of a perfect network has all of the computers hooked up to each other, with no humans present, in a room that's locked from the inside.

With that caution, it's probably worthwhile to consult with a security expert to assess your specific needs and install a system that meets those needs, but stays within your budget.

5. The shopping cart application

Now that you have the entire infrastructure in place, you're ready to consider a shopping cart application to bring it all together. You can either extend the online catalogue you've already established in Project 22, or you can implement a commercial shopping cart application off the shelf.

A shopping cart is generally comprised of a number of elements, all of which must work together. First, there must be some way for the customer to indicate which items he or she is interested in, and in what quantities. This usually incorporates a page where the customer can review the items chosen so far, and make adjustments.

Next, there's the checkout process, where the customer provides any necessary shipment information, and then moves on to payment arrangements. Typically, payment options are simply credit cards, but your business model may require that you accept purchase orders or extended payment terms of some sort.

Finally, there should be some sort of order confirmation. This is typically emailed to the customer, and should usually include all of the order details, including items ordered, shipping instructions, and payment arrangements. If you include an order number, this will be useful if your customers want to contact you regarding the order.

As an added step, you may wish to send a follow-on message with any available shipment tracking information. This will save you a lot of calls and emails, particularly if there are delays in shipping beyond your control.

A basic design feature of shopping carts is whether they store the information of a transaction currently in progress on the customer's computer, or on your server. If the information is stored on the customer's system, this is typically accomplished by the use of "cookies." Cookies, despite their negative reputation, are simply a means for you to store a small amount of information on your customer's computer that you can then refer back to later.

Unfortunately, because of the bad reputation that this technology has gotten, some customers will disable cookies – which would mean that they couldn't shop on your site, if you've chosen this technology to manage your shopping cart.

On the other hand, storing all of the information about the order as it's being built on your Web server requires some more so-phisticated software, since you need to ensure that you don't mix details from one customer's order with another customer's. Your Web manager can discuss the pros and cons of these technologies with you and help you to make a decision.

If you'll be simply extending your existing product catalogue pages, you should add to each product detail page a means for the customer to order that item. What seems to work well is a simple "buy me now" or "add to cart" button, followed by a means for the customer to change quantities on the order summary page. Alternatively, you could include a quantity selector on the detail page.

On the order summary page, you should give the customer a means to return to the product catalogue, so that he or she can add on other items to the order. An advanced order summary screen implementation might even suggest add-on products that the customer can select directly from there.

When it's time for checkout, the information required will depend upon your business needs. Bear in mind that most shipping companies will not ship to post office box, APO or FPO addresses, so you must have a physical address from your customer if you will be shipping a package of some sort.

When it's time to collect payment information, if you'll be taking credit card payments, you can either have your site hand processing over to a third-party processor's site (such as PayPal), or you can collect the information yourself. If you will be collecting credit card data, you *must* now switch over to a secured page. Not all customers are savvy enough to look for the SSL icon in their browser, but the liability for accepting credit card information "in the clear" could be costly.

You will probably want to implement some sort of card number validation, even if you'll be processing payments with your existing merchant agreement and card processing systems. There are a number of publicly available routines that verify that, at the very least, you have a credit card number that could have been issued at some point.

If you're working with an online credit card processor, they will have provided you with the necessary details to integrate their capabilities into your systems. Consult them for any additional assistance that you may require. Remember that you should always transmit credit card data via a secured system.

Once the payment's handled, you should provide a page that details what they've ordered, where it will be shipped, and how they paid for it. Of course, do not transmit their credit card number in this summary. You may want to send similar information to the customer via email. (You *did* get their email address, right? And asked permission to contact them in the future? Good!)

Of course, if you're not interested in reinventing the wheel, there are a lot of good pre-built shopping carts out there. Look for one that is compatible with your Web server, unless you're willing to establish a separate server for this application. You may want to look at osCommerce, at www.oscommerce.com, MivaMerchant, at www.miva.com, ShopSite at www.shopsite.com and PDG Shopping Cart, at www.pdgsoft.com.

Some of these shopping cart applications are available as a hosted package, where the software vendor (or a partner of theirs) actually hosts the system, and you just link into it. See Project 24 for more information about this model of Web site software.

There are literally dozens of entrants in this market, so this list is necessarily incomplete. A check of your favorite search engine for the terms "shopping cart software" or "e-commerce solutions" will give you other vendors to look at, as well.

Some of the features that may be important in your business include the ability to offer "preferred customer" discounts, gift certificate redemption, integration with your other business software systems, multi-jurisdictional tax management, shipment tracking integration, inventory import and traffic reporting.

Once you have implemented a shopping cart application, you will need to establish processes to keep your inventory synchronized between your Web site and any offline applications that you may be using. This will prevent customers from ordering products that you no longer have, and will also permit you to make more informed re-stocking decisions.

Having a full-blown e-commerce site will change the way that you do business. Even if you've done mail order in the past, you will now have the ability to reach a broader audience than ever. Most importantly, your customers will benefit from the convenience of anytime, anywhere availability of your products and services.

Assessing Results

Look at overall sales volume, and watch to ensure that the overhead of establishing an e-commerce site doesn't outstrip the benefits of the additional volume. Your business's geographic reach will probably be extended by the addition of e-commerce, and your customer referrals will probably rise, as well – it's exceptionally easy to send someone a Web site for a great provider of a product or service that you use.

What's Next?

With an e-commerce site, it's more important than ever to have a firm handle on your Web site traffic. You need to be very sure that the design and performance of your site continually supports the success of your shopping cart. If you haven't already done so, go through Project 11 to establish a routine of analyzing your Web site traffic.

Project 24:
Using Hosted Business Software

There are many classes of business software, such as payroll, finance, customer relationship management and so on, that have previously been available only to very large businesses, with hefty investments in infrastructure.

Many of these systems are available now to small businesses through ASPs ("application service providers"), without the need to perform complex installations, available anywhere you can get an Internet connection and for which someone else takes care of the maintenance. The availability of this sort of software can literally change the way you do business.

Prerequisites

You must have Internet access, preferably high-speed, always-on access, as discussed in Project 12.

Cost projections

Typically, for each application that you decide to use in a hosted environment, there will be a startup fee, which will cover loading your initial data, any customizations that you might need and setting up your PC to use the software. This fee will vary widely, depending on the complexity of these tasks. Budget from $1,000 to $10,000 – but consult with the ASP for a closer approximation.

Each application will have a usage fee, as well, usually charged on a monthly, per-user basis. A very few applications are free, but most cost in the range of $100 to $500 per month, per user.

Goals

If you're already using an application of the sort that you select on your own servers, you should be able to reduce your IT costs – or use your IT resources for more important tasks. If the implementation costs and complexity have prevented you from using a particular type of application, this project will yield the benefits of now being able to access far more powerful software than you could previously.

Procedures

1. Understanding the technology

Hosted applications are, in a way, a very old concept. In the early days of the computer revolution, very few computer users actually had a computer on their desks. By and large, they had "dumb terminals," which simply displayed what a large, expensive computer was doing, and accepted input to that computer. The real computer would be shared between many users, allowing them to share in the costs of maintaining the entire system.

ASP hosted software uses the exact same metaphor – only now, you use a browser, instead of a dumb terminal to access the central computer. The browser is a lot more capable than a terminal was, but the bulk of the work is still being done on the central computer.

There are a number of models being used in the ASP market today, each of which is well suited to a particular type of application. The primary difference you will notice between the models is in how much specialized software you must load on your computer in order to use them.

Some ASPs host software using a system that basically runs a complete Microsoft Windows or UNIX session, and then gives you remote access to it. In this sort of solution, you can run nearly any software that you could run on your own computer, but it actually lives on the ASP's machines.

In theory, you could run anything from your basic office software, on up to enterprise management suites in this environment. In practice, unless you have a very fast Internet connection, you will want to continue running word processors, spreadsheets and so forth on your own computers, and use the ASP-hosted systems for the specialized, complex packages.

Your browser will have to load a plug-in, which is a piece of specialized software installed on your machine, in order to access this sort of hosted system. Typically, the application will appear completely within this plug-in, which can appear in your browser, or as standalone software.

Other ASPs have packages that do not create an entire desktop session on the ASP's machine, but just runs the specific software you're using. In order to manage security, communications, or some specialized display functions, these systems may also require you to load a plug-in – but the difference is that the application runs in your browser, and simply uses the plug-in for some tasks.

Typically, this sort of software is well suited for applications that can present and accept most of their information in a standard browser interface, but for which you may have a need for high security, or for complex display capabilities, such as graphing. Many Web site traffic tools are available under this hosting model.

Finally, some ASP-provided systems can run in a pure browser environment, requiring no software installation on your computer at all. These can be very convenient to access when you're traveling, in particular. A Web-hosted email account is a very common example of a solution in this class, as are hosted e-commerce solutions.

Security can be provided in this hosting model by using SSL encryption (see Project 4 for a complete discussion of how SSL works) between the hosting system and your browser.

2. Investigate the offerings

There are hosted solutions in nearly any class of business software that you can imagine. Some of the most common include human resource management (including payroll, recruiting and employee reviews), finance and accounting, customer relationship management (including sales automation and customer support management) and enterprise resource management (including inventory, procurement, travel arrangements and supply chain management).

You will also find a large number of collaboration tools available in a hosted environment. These include Web-based email, discussion groups, online chat systems and hosted whiteboard applications.

The place where nearly all business applications incur their greatest expense is in implementation – which usually means customization. As you look at hosted solutions, keep an eye out for places where you feel that you just wouldn't be able to live with the way it is "out of the box." No matter what the salesperson tells you, customization will be the most costly and risky thing that you do.

This is not to say that you have to find an application that matches your exact needs, with no variations. However, you should ask yourself whether a given change is completely necessary to your business. The concept of the "80-20" rule applies here: 80% of your effort will be expended on changing the 20% of the application that you feel doesn't meet your needs. Unless that 20% is truly critical, save the 80% effort for learning the application, loading your data, and rolling it out to your organization.

An excellent site for looking into the range of offerings on the ASP market is www.asp-directory.com. You can also go to your favorite search engine and use the search term "ASP" in addition to the type of software you're after – "payroll ASP" for example.

3. Before you sign on the dotted line...

Once you've found an ASP package that you want to integrate into your business, you'll typically have some sort of implementation process. This may be as simple as just loading a few pieces of critical data by hand, or it might involve a complex data import, customization, and software installation on your machines. Find out exactly what this process will entail, and exactly how much you'll spend.

Be sure to ask whether any customizations that you do perform will continue to work as underlying application is upgraded. Check into the stability of the hosting company itself – the last thing that you want is for your business-critical application to disappear, along with your highly valuable data. Be sure that the contract includes provisions for the privacy and security of your data.

As your business grows, you'll also want the assurance of knowing that the solution you choose can grow with you. Be sure that you can add users at a reasonable cost, and find out what the limits are. Find out, too, what limits exist as far as the volume of information that the system can handle. An accounting system that can only deal with a few thousand customers may be fine for today, but what about three years from now?

If you will be licensing the system for multiple users, is it licensed per named user, or per concurrent user? Are there fees associated with larger volumes of data? How long can you lock in your pricing?

If you need to migrate to another solution in the future, how hard will it be to export your data? Can you perform local backups of your data? What sort of backup systems and procedures are in place at the vendor? Do they have an offsite recovery plan, in case of a major disaster?

Obviously, the answers to these questions are not the only thing that you should consider. Expense and fit to your needs are also important factors. You should weigh all of these, and consider, too, whether you could save money over the long run by implementing a solution in house.

Once you have satisfied yourself about these considerations, though, you will likely find that ASP hosted solutions open the door to a range of business automation and management tools that were previously only available to the largest enterprises. Having the power of these solutions at your fingertips will enable you to enjoy the same advantages that only larger business have until now.

Assessing Results

By sharing the costs of system maintenance, software licensing, and implementation with other customers, you should be able to dramatically reduce your month-to-month expenses for business software. Alternatively, if you're gaining access to solutions that were previously out of reach, you should be able to do more, without having to add a lot of overhead staff to implement and maintain these systems.

What's Next?

This project can serve as your guide to implementing a number of different business solutions. As you've become more familiar with hosted software, you'll notice that many of the other projects in this book can be supported with ASP-based solutions.

In both Projects 22 and 23, you will find that there are strong solutions that involve hosted applications to manage your e-commerce needs. As mentioned in Project 11, some of the leading analysis tools on the market are available as hosted solutions.

Appendix A:
Suggested Reading

Each of these books is entertaining, insightful and will give you new ideas to extend the projects you've undertaken in this book. All of these are available from Amazon.com, BN.com and so on, and most should be available at your local bookseller.

Flynn, Nancy, Tom Flynn. *Writing Effective Email: Improving Your Electronic Communication.* Menlo Park, California: Crisp Publications, 1998.

Johnson, Jeff. *Web Bloopers: 60 Common Web Design Mistakes and How to Avoid Them.* San Francisco, California: Morgan Kaufmann Publishers, 2003.

Kawasaki, Guy. *How to Drive Your Competition Crazy: Creating Disruption for Fun and Profit.* New York: Hyperion, 1995.

Krug, Steve, Black, Roger. *Don't Make Me Think: A Common Sense Approach to Web Usability.* Indianapolis, Indiana: New Riders, 2000.

Locke, Christopher, Rick Levine, Doc Searls, David Weinberger. *The Cluetrain Manifesto: The End of Business as Usual.* Cambridge, Massachusetts: Perseus Books, 2001.

Siegel, David. *Futurize Your Enterprise: Business Strategy in the Age of the E-customer.* New York: John Wiley & Sons, 1999.

Vitale, Joe. *Cyber Writing: How to Promote Your Product or Service Online (Without Being Flamed).* New York: Amacom, 1997.

Appendix B:
Online Resources

Search Engines
> www.google.com
> www.altavista.com
> www.hotbot.com
> www.ask.com
> www.mamma.com

Web Directories
> www.yahoo.com
> directory.google.com

Web-Based email
> www.gmail.com
> www.hotmail.com
> mail.yahoo.com

Domain Registrars
> www.godaddy.com
> www.register.com
> www.networksolutions.com

Site Hosting
> www.definitivehosting.com
> www.hostforadollar.com
> www.freeservers.com
> angelfire.lycos.com

Web Site Index

www.ingramcontent.com/pod-product-compliance
Lightning Source LLC
Chambersburg PA
CBHW051236050326
40689CB00007B/945

9 781420 874549